Freemasons and Rosicrucians
The Enlightened

by Manly P. Hall

Edited by Michael R. Poll

Freemasons and Rosicrucians - The Enlightened
by Manly P. Hall
Edited by Michael R. Poll

A Cornerstone Book
Published by Cornerstone Book Publishers
Copyright © 2005, 2013, & 2024 as a collection by Michael R. Poll

All rights reserved under International and Pan-American Copyright Conventions. No part of this book may be reproduced in any manner without permission in writing from the copyright holder, except by a reviewer, who may quote brief passages in a review.

Cornerstone Book Publishers
Hot Springs Village, AR
www.cornerstonepublishers.com

First Cornerstone Edition – 2005
Second Cornerstone Edition – 2013
Third Cornerstone Edition – 2024

Foreword

Manly Palmer Hall (1901-1990) taught, inspired, and served as a beacon for countless numbers on their path towards Light. The author of over 200 books and thousands of articles, Manly Hall was honored in 1990 (shortly before his death) with the 33rd degree of the Ancient and Accepted Scottish Rite of Freemasonry – the highest degree in this system of Masonry. As one who often portrayed himself as a student, he was truly an enlightened guide.

The collection of essays offered in this work were written in the 1920's, but the Masonic and Rosicrucian philosophy presented could well have been written in the 1720's or 2020's. It is a timeless, insightful philosophy that provides us with a glimpse into a reality that so few can properly master.

A study of these works is not only beneficial for Freemasons and Rosicrucians, but offers us all a chance to grow, evolve, and develop. From the sage words of Manly Hall, we can better understand the motives, methods, and practices of the initiated and Seekers of Light.

With all wishes for Peace Profound.

Michael R. Poll
2005

Table of Contents

Foreword vii
Rosicrucian and Masonic Origins 1
The Hiramic Legend 23
The Lost Keys of Freemasonry 41
    Prologue - In the Fields of Chaos 46
    Chapter I - The Eternal Quest 52
    Chapter II - The Candidate 58
    Chapter III - The Entered Apprentice 63
    Chapter IV - The Fellow Craft 69
    Chapter V - The Master Mason 74
    Chapter VI - The Qualifications of a True Mason 79
    Epilogue - The Priest of Ra 85
Freemasonic Symbolism 93
The Fraternity of the Rose Cross 109
Rosicrucian Doctrines and Tenets 127

Freemasons and Rosicrucians
The Enlightened

Rosicrucian and Masonic Origins
(1929)

FREEMASONRY is a fraternity within a fraternity—an outer organization concealing an inner brotherhood of the elect. Before it is possible to intelligently discuss the origin of the Craft, it is necessary, therefore, to establish the existence of these two separate yet interdependent orders, the one visible and the other invisible. The visible society is a splendid *camaraderie* of "free and accepted" men enjoined to devote themselves to ethical, educational, fraternal, patriotic, and humanitarian concerns. The invisible society is a secret and most august fraternity whose members are dedicated to the service of a mysterious *arcanum arcanorum*. Those Brethren who have essayed to write the history of their Craft have not included in their disquisitions the story of that truly secret inner society which is to the body Freemasonic what the heart is to the body human. In each generation only a few are accepted into the inner sanctuary of the Work, but these are veritable Princes of the Truth, and their sainted names shall be remembered in future ages together with the seers and prophets of the elder world. Though the great initiate-philosophers of Freemasonry can be counted upon one's fingers, yet their power is not to be measured by the achievements of ordinary men. They are dwellers upon the Threshold of the Innermost, Masters of that secret doctrine which forms the invisible foundation of every great theological and rational institution.

The outer history of the Masonic order is one of noble endeavor, altruism, and splendid enterprise; the inner history, one of silent conquest, persecution, and heroic martyrdom. The body of Masonry rose from the guilds of workmen who wandered the face of medieval Europe, but the spirit of Masonry walked with God before the universe was spread out or the scroll of the heavens unrolled. The enthusiasm of the young Mason is the effervescence of a pardonable pride. Let him extol the merits of his Craft, reciting its steady growth, its fraternal spirit, and its worthy undertakings. Let him boast of splendid buildings and an ever-increasing sphere of influence. These are the tangible evidence of power and should rightly set fluttering the heart of the Apprentice who does not fully comprehend as yet that great strength which abides in silence or that unutterable dignity to be sensed only by those who. have been "raised" into the contemplation of the Inner Mystery.

An obstacle well-nigh insurmountable is to convince the Mason himself that the secrets of his Craft are worthy of his profound consideration. As St. Paul, so we are told, kicked against the "pricks" of conversion, so the rank and file of present-day Masons strenuously oppose any effort put forth to interpret Masonic symbols in the light of philosophy. They are seemingly obsessed by the fear that from their ritualism may be extracted a meaning more profound than is actually contained therein. For years it has been a moot question whether Freemasonry is actually a religious organization. "Masonry," writes Pike, however, in the *Legenda for the Nineteenth Degree*, "has and always had a religious creed. It teaches what it deems to be the truth in respect to the nature and attributes of God." The more studiously-minded Mason regards the Craft as an aggregation of thinkers concerned with the deeper mysteries of life. The all-too-prominent younger members of the Fraternity, however, if not openly skeptical, are at least indifferent to these weightier issues. The champions of philosophic Masonry, alas, are a weak, small voice which grows weaker and smaller as time goes by. In fact, there are actual blocs among the Brethren who would divorce Masonry from both philosophy and religion at any and all cost. If, however, we search the writings of eminent Masons, we find a unanimity of viewpoint: namely, that Masonry is a religious and philosophic body. Every effort initiated to elevate Masonic thought to its true position has thus invariably emphasized the metaphysical and ethical aspects of the Craft.

But a superficial perusal of available documents will demonstrate that the modern Masonic order is not united respecting the true purpose for its own existence. Nor will this factor of doubt be dispelled until the origin of the Craft is established beyond all quibbling. The elements of Masonic history are strangely elusive; there are gaps which apparently cannot be bridged. "Who the early Freemasons really were," states Gould in *A Concise History of Freemasonry*, "and whence they came, may afford a tempting theme for inquiry to the speculative antiquary. But it is enveloped in obscurity, and lies far outside the domain of authentic history." Between modern Freemasonry with its vast body of ancient symbolism and those original Mysteries which first employed these symbols there is a dark interval of centuries. To the conservative Masonic historian, the deductions of such writers as Higgins, Churchward, Vail, and Waite—though ingenious and fascinating—actually prove nothing. That Masonry is a body of ancient lore is self-evident, but the tangible "link" necessary to convince the recalcitrant Brethren that their order is the direct successor of the pagan Mysteries has unfortunately not been adduced to date. Of such problems as these is composed the "angel" with which the Masonic Jacob must wrestle throughout the night.

It is possible to trace Masonry back a few centuries with comparative ease, but then the thread suddenly vanishes from sight in a maze of secret societies and political enterprises. Dimly silhouetted in the mists that becloud these tangled issues are such figures as Cagliostro, Comte de St. Germain, and St. Martin, but even the connection between these individuals and the Craft has never been clearly defined. The writing of early Masonic history is involved in such obvious hazard as to provoke the widespread conclusion that further search is futile. The average Masonic student is content, therefore, to trace his Craft back to the workmen's guilds who chipped and chiseled the cathedrals and public buildings of medieval Europe. While such men as

Albert Pike have realized this attitude to be ridiculous, it is one thing to declare it insufficient and quite another to prove the fallacy to an adamantine mind. So much has been lost and forgotten, so much ruled in and out by those unfitted for such legislative revision that the modern rituals do not in every case represent the original rites of the Craft. In his *Symbolism*, Pike (who spent a lifetime in the quest for Masonic secrets) declares that few of the original meanings of the symbols are known to the modern order, nearly all the so-called interpretations now given being superficial. Pike confessed that the original meanings of the very symbols he himself was attempting to interpret were irretrievably lost; that even such familiar emblems as the apron and the pillars were locked mysteries, whose "keys" had been thrown away by the uninformed. "The initiated," also writes John Fellows, "as well as those without the pale of the order, are equally ignorant of their derivation and import. (See: *The Mysteries of Freemasonry*.)

Preston, Gould, Mackey, Oliver, and Pike—in fact, nearly every great historian of Freemasonry—have all admitted the possibility of the modern society being connected, indirectly at least, with the ancient Mysteries, and their descriptions of the modern society are prefaced by excerpts from ancient writings descriptive of primitive ceremonials. These eminent Masonic scholars have all recognized in the legend of Hiram Abiff an adaptation of the Osiris myth; nor do they deny that the major part of the symbolism of the craft is derived from the pagan institutions of antiquity when the gods were venerated in secret places with strange figures and appropriate rituals. Though cognizant of the exalted origin of their order, these historians—either through fear or uncertainty—have failed, however, to drive home the one point necessary to establish the true purpose of Freemasonry: *They did not realize that the Mysteries whose rituals Freemasonry perpetuates were the custodians of a secret philosophy of life of such transcendent nature that it can only be entrusted to an individual tested and proved beyond all peradventure of human frailty.* The secret schools of Greece and Egypt were neither fraternal nor political fundamentally, nor were their ideals similar to those of the modern Craft. They were essentially philosophic and religious institutions, and all admitted into them were consecrated to the service of the sovereign good. Modern Freemasons, however, regard their Craft primarily as neither philosophic nor religious, but rather as ethical. Strange as it may seem, the majority openly ridicule the very supernatural powers and agencies for which their symbols stand.

The secret doctrine that flows through Freemasonic symbols (and to whose perpetuation the invisible Masonic body is consecrated) has its source in three ancient and exalted orders. The first is the Dionysiac artificers, the second the Roman *collegia*, and the third the Arabian Rosicrucians. The Dionysians were the master builders of the ancient world. Originally founded to design and erect the theaters of Dionysos wherein were enacted the tragic dramas of the rituals, this order was repeatedly elevated by popular acclaim to greater dignity until at last it was entrusted with the planning and construction of all public edifices concerned with the commonwealth or the worship of the gods and heroes. Hiram, King of Tyre, was the patron of the Dionysians, who flourished in Tyre and Sidon, and Hiram Abiff (if we may believe the sacred account) was himself a Grand Master of this most noble order of pagan builders. King Solomon in his wisdom accepted the services of this famous craftsman, and thus at the instigation of Hiram, King of Tyre, Hiram Abiff, though himself a member of a different faith, journeyed from his own country to design and supervise the erection of the Everlasting House to the true God on Mount Moriah. The tools of the builders' craft were first employed by the Dionysians as symbols under which to conceal the mysteries of the soul and the secrets of human regeneration. The Dionysians also first likened man to a rough *ashlar* which, trued into a finished block through the instrument of reason, could be fitted into the structure of that living and eternal Temple built without the sound of hammer, the voice of workmen or any tool of contention.

The Roman *collegia* was a branch of the Dionysiacs and to it belonged those initiated artisans who fashioned the impressive monuments whose ruins still lend their immortal glory to the Eternal City. In his *Ten Books on Architecture*, Vitruvius, the initiate of the *collegia*, has revealed that which was permissible concerning the secrets of his holy order. Of the inner mysteries, however, he could not write, for these were reserved for such as had donned the leather apron of the craft. In his consideration of the books now available concerning the Mysteries, the thoughtful reader should note the following words appearing in a twelfth-century volume entitled *Artephil Liber Secretus*: "Is not this an art full of secrets? And believest thou, O fool! that we plainly teach this Secret of Secrets, taking our words according to their literal interpretation?" (See: *Sephar H' Debarim*) Into the stones they trued, the adepts of the *collegia* deeply carved their Gnostic symbols. From earliest times, the initiated stonecutters marked their perfected works with the secret emblems of their crafts and degrees that unborn generations might realize that the master builders of the first ages also labored for the same ends sought by men today.

The Mysteries of Egypt and Persia that had found a haven in the Arabian desert reached Europe by way of the Knights Templars and the Rosicrucians. The Temple of the Rose Cross at Damascus had preserved the secret philosophy of Sharon's Rose; the Druses of the Lebanon still retain the mysticism of ancient Syria; and the dervishes, as they lean on their carved and crotched sticks, still meditate upon the secret instruction perpetuated from the days of the four Caliphs. From the far places of Iraq and the hidden retreats of the Sufi mystics, the Ancient Wisdom thus found its way into Europe. Was Jacques de Molay burned by the Holy Inquisition merely because he wore the red cross of the Templar? What were those secrets to which he was true even in death? Did his companion Knights perish with him merely because they had amassed a fortune and exercised an unusual degree of temporal power? To the thoughtless, these may constitute ample grounds, but to those who can pierce the film of the specious and the superficial, they are assuredly insufficient. It was not the physical power of the Templars but the knowledge which they had brought with them from the East that the church feared. The Templars had discovered part of the Great Arcanum; they had become wise in those mysteries which had been celebrated in Mecca thousands of years before the advent of Mohammed; they had read a few pages from the dread book of the Anthropos, and for this knowledge they were doomed to die. What was the black magic of which the Templars were accused? What was Baphomet, the Goat of Mendes, whose mysteries they were declared to have celebrated? All these are questions worthy of the thoughtful consideration of every studious Mason.

Truth is eternal. The so-called revelations of Truth that come in different religions are actually but a re-emphasis of an ever-existing doctrine. Thus, Moses did not originate a new religion for Israel; he simply adapted the Mysteries of Egypt to the needs of Israel. The ark triumphantly borne by the twelve tribes through the wilderness was copied after the Isiac ark which may still be traced in faint relief upon the ruins of the Temple of Philae. Even the two brooding cherubim over the mercy seat are visible in the Egyptian carving, furnishing indubitable evidence that the secret doctrine of Egypt was the prototype of Israel's mystery religion. In his reformation of Indian philosophy, Buddha likewise did not reject the esotericism of the Brahmins, but rather adapted this esotericism to the needs of the masses in India. The mystic secrets locked within the holy Vedas were thus disclosed in order that all men, irrespective of caste distinction, might partake of wisdom and share in a common heritage of good. Jesus was a Rabbin of the Jews, a teacher of the Holy Law, who discoursed in the synagogue, interpreting the Torah according to the teachings of His sect. He brought no new message nor were His reformations radical. He merely tore away the veil from the temple in order that not only Pharisee and Sadducee but also publican and sinner might together behold the glory of an ageless faith.

In his cavern on Mount Hira, Mohammed prayed not for new truths but for old truths to be restated in their original purity and simplicity in order that men might understand again that primitive religion: God's clear revelation to the first patriarchs. The Mysteries of Islam had been celebrated in the great black cube of the Kaaba centuries before the holy pilgrimage. The Prophet was but the reformer of a decadent pagandom, the smasher of idols, the purifier of defiled Mysteries. The dervishes, who patterned their garments after those of the Prophet, still preserve that inner teaching of the elect, and for them the *Axis of the Earth* —the supreme hierophant—still sits, visible only to the faithful, in meditation upon the flat roof of the Kaaba. Neither carpenter nor camel-driver, as Abdul Baha might have said, can fashion a world religion from the substances of his own mind. Neither prophet nor savior preached a doctrine which was his own, but in language suitable to his time and race retold that Ancient Wisdom preserved within the Mysteries since the dawning of human consciousness. So with the Masonic Mysteries of today. Each Mason has at hand those lofty principles of universal order upon whose certainties the faiths of mankind have ever been established. Each Mason has at hand those lofty principles of universal order upon pregnant with life and hope to those millions who wander in the darkness of unenlightenment.

Father C.R.C., the Master of the Rose Cross, was initiated into the Great Work at Damcar. Later at Fez, further information was given him relating to the sorcery of the Arabians. From these wizards of the desert C.R.C. also secured the sacred book M, which is declared to have contained the accumulated knowledge of the world. This volume was translated into Latin by C.R.C. for the edification of his order, but only the initiates know the present hidden repository of the Rosicrucian manuscripts, charters, and manifestos. From the Arabians C.R.C. also learned of the elemental peoples and how, with their aid, it was possible to gain admission to the ethereal world where dwelt the genii and Nature spirits. C.R.C. thus discovered that the magical creatures of the *Arabian Nights Entertainment* actually existed, though invisible to the ordinary mortal. From astrologers living in the desert far from the concourse of the market-place he was further instructed concerning the mysteries of the stars, the virtues resident in the astral light, the rituals of magic and invocation, the preparation of therapeutic talismans, and the binding of the genii. C.R.C. became an adept in the gathering of medicinal herbs, the transmutation of metals, and the manufacture of precious gems by artificial means. Even the secret of the Elixir of Life and the Universal Panacea were communicated to him. Enriched thus beyond the dreams of Croesus, the Holy Master returned to Europe and there established a House of Wisdom which he called *Domus Sancti Spiritus*. This house he enveloped in clouds, it is said, so that men could not discover it. What are these "clouds," however, but the rituals and symbols under which is concealed the Great Arcanum—that unspeakable mystery which every true Mason must seek if he would become in reality a "Prince of the Royal Secret"?

Paracelsus, the Swiss Hermes, was initiated into the secrets of alchemy in Constantinople and there beheld the consummation of the *magnum opus*. He is consequently entitled to be mentioned among those initiated by the Arabians into the Rosicrucian work. Cagliostro was also initiated by the Arabians and, because of the knowledge he had thus secured, incurred the displeasure of the Holy See. From the unprobed depths of Arabian Rosicrucianism also issued the illustrious Comte de St. Germain, over whose Masonic activities to this day hangs the veil of impenetrable mystery. The exalted body of initiates whom he represented, as well as the mission he came to accomplish, have both been concealed from the members of the Craft at large and are apparent only to those few discerning Masons who sense the supernal philosophic destiny of their Fraternity.

The modern Masonic order can be traced back to a period in European history famous for its intrigue both political and sociological. Between the years 1600 and 1800, mysterious agents moved across the face of the Continent. The forerunner of modern thought was beginning to make its appearance and all Europe was passing through the throes of internal dissension and reconstruction. Democracy was in its infancy, yet its potential power was already being felt. Thrones were beginning to totter. The aristocracy of Europe was like the old man on Sinbad's back: it was becoming more unbearable with every passing day. Although upon the surface national governments were seemingly able to cope with the situation, there was a definite undercurrent of impending change; and out of the masses, long patient under the yoke of oppression, were rising up the champions of religious, philosophic, and political liberty. These led the factions of the dissatisfied: people with legitimate grievances against the intolerance of the church and the oppression of the crown. Out of this struggle for expression materialized certain definite ideals, the same which have now come to be considered peculiarly Masonic.

The divine prerogatives of humanity were being crushed out by the three great powers of ignorance, superstition, and fear—ignorance, the power of the mob; fear, the power of the despot; and superstition, the power of the church. Between the thinker and personal liberty loomed the three "ruffians" or personifications of impediment—the torch, the crown, and the tiara. Brute force, kingly power, and ecclesiastical persuasion became the agents of a great oppression, the motive of a deep unrest, the deterrent to all progress. It was unlawful to think, well-nigh fatal to philosophize, rank heresy to doubt. To question the infallibility of the existing order was to invite the persecution of the church and the state. These together incited the populace, which thereupon played the role of executioner for these archenemies of human liberty. Thus, the ideal of democracy assumed a definite form during these stormy periods of European history. This democracy was not only a vision but a retrospection, not only a looking forward but a gazing backward upon better days and the effort to project those better days into the unborn tomorrow. The ethical, political, and philosophical institutions of antiquity with their constructive effect upon the whole structure of the state were noble examples of possible conditions. It became the dream of the oppressed, consequently, to re-establish a golden age upon the earth, an age where the thinker could think in safety and the dreamer dream in peace; when the wise should lead and the simple follow, yet all dwell together in fraternity and industry.

During this period several books were in circulation which, to a certain degree, registered the pulse of the time. One of these documents—More's *Utopia*—was the picture of a new age when heavenly conditions should prevail upon the earth. This ideal of establishing good in the world savored of blasphemy, however, for in that day heaven alone it was assumed could be good. Men did not seek to establish heavenly conditions upon earth, but rather earthly conditions in heaven. According to popular concept, the more the individual suffered the torments of the damned upon earth, the more he would enjoy the blessedness of heaven. Life was a period of chastisement and earthly happiness an unattainable mirage. More's *Utopia* thus came as a definite blow to autocratic pretensions and attitudes, giving impulse to the material emphasis which was to follow in succeeding centuries.

Another prominent figure of this period was Sir Walter Raleigh, who paid with his life for high treason against the crown. Raleigh was tried and, though the charge was never proved, was executed. Before Raleigh went to trial, it was known that he must die and that no defense could save him. His treason against the crown was of a character very different, however, from that which history records. Raleigh was a member of a secret society or body of men who were already moving irresistibly forward under the banner of democracy, and for that affiliation he died a felon's death. The actual reason for Raleigh's death sentence was his refusal to reveal the identity either of that great political organization of which he was a member or his confreres who were fighting the dogma of faith and the divine right of kings. On the title page of the first edition of Raleigh's *History of the World*, we accordingly find a mass of intricate emblems framed between two great columns. When the executioner sealed his lips forever, Raleigh's silence, while it added to the discomfiture of his persecutors, assured the safety of his colleagues.

One of the truly great minds of that secret fraternity—in fact, the moving spirit of the whole enterprise—was Sir Francis Bacon, whose prophecy of the coming age forms the theme of his *New Atlantis* and whose vision of the reformation of knowledge finds expression in the *Novum Organum Scientiarum*, the new organ of science or thought. In the engraving at the beginning of the latter volume may be seen the little ship of progressivism sailing out between the Pillars of Galen and Avicenna, venturing forth beyond the imaginary pillars of church and state upon the unknown sea of human liberty. It is significant that Bacon was appointed by the British Crown to protect its interests in the new American Colonies beyond the sea. We find him writing of this new land, dreaming of the day when a new world and a new government of the philosophic elect should be established there, and scheming to consummate that end when the time should be ripe. Upon the title page of the 1640 edition of Bacon's *Advancement of Learning* is a Latin motto to the effect that he was the third great mind since Plato. Bacon was a member of the same group to which Sir Walter Raleigh belonged, but Bacon's position as Lord High Chancellor protected him from Raleigh's fate. Every effort was made, however, to humiliate and discredit him. At last, in the sixty-sixth year of his life, having completed the work which held him in England, Bacon feigned death and passed over into Germany, there to guide the destinies of his philosophic and political fraternity for nearly twenty-five years before his actual demise.

Other notable characters of the period are Montaigne, Ben Jonson, Marlowe, and the great Franz Joseph of Transylvania—the latter one of the most important as well as active figures in all this drama, a man who ceased fighting Austria to retire into a monastery in Transylvania from which to direct the activities of his secret society. One political upheaval followed another, the grand climax of this political unrest culminating in the French Revolution, which was directly precipitated by the attacks upon the person of Alessandro Cagliostro. The "divine" Cagliostro, by far the most picturesque character of the time, has the distinction of being more maligned than any other person of history. Tried by the Inquisition for founding a Masonic lodge in the city of Rome, Cagliostro was sentenced to die, a sentence later commuted by the Pope to life imprisonment in the old castle of San Leo. Shortly after his incarceration, Cagliostro disappeared, and the story was circulated that he had been strangled in an attempt to escape from prison. In reality, however, he was liberated and returned to his Masters in the East. But Cagliostro—the idol of France, surnamed "the Father of the Poor," who never received anything from anyone and gave everything to everyone—was most adequately revenged. Though the people little understood this inexhaustible pitcher of bounty which poured forth benefits and never required replenishment, they remembered him in the day of their power.

Cagliostro founded the Egyptian Rite of Freemasonry, which received into its mysteries many of the French nobility and was regarded favorably by the most learned minds of Europe. Having established the Egyptian Rite, Cagliostro declared himself to be an agent of the order of the Knights Templars and to have received initiation from them on the Isle of Malta. (See: *Morals and Dogma*, in which Albert Pike quotes Eliphas Levi on Cagliostro's affiliation with the Templars.) Called upon the carpet by the Supreme Council of France, it was demanded of Cagliostro that he prove by what authority he had founded a Masonic lodge in Paris independent of the Grand Orient. Of such surpassing mentality was Cagliostro that the Supreme Council found it difficult to secure an advocate qualified to discuss with Cagliostro philosophic Masonry and the ancient Mysteries he claimed to represent. The Court de Gebelin—the greatest Egyptologist of his day and an authority on ancient philosophies-was chosen as the outstanding scholar. A time was set and the Brethren convened. Attired in an Oriental coat and a pair of violet-colored breeches, Cagliostro was haled before this council of his peers. The Court de Gebelin asked three questions and then sat down, admitting himself disqualified to interrogate a man so much his superior in every branch of learning. Cagliostro then took the floor, revealing to the assembled Masons not only his personal qualifications, but prophesying the future of France. He foretold the fall of the French throne, the Reign of Terror, and the fall of the Bastille. At a later time he revealed the dates of the death of Marie Antoinette and the King, and also the advent of Napoleon. Having finished his address, Cagliostro made a spectacular exit, leaving the French Masonic lodge in consternation and utterly incapable of coping with the profundity of his reasoning. Though no longer regarded as a ritual in Freemasonry, the Egyptian Rite is available and all who read it will recognize its author to have been no more a charlatan than was Plato.

Then appears that charming "first American gentleman," Dr. Benjamin Franklin, who together with the Marquis de Lafayette, played an important role in this drama of empires. While in France, Dr. Franklin was privileged to receive definite esoteric instruction. It is noteworthy that Franklin was the first in America to reprint Anderson's *Constitutions of the Free-Masons*, which is a most prized work on the subject, though its accuracy is disputed. Through all this stormy period, these impressive figures come and go, part of a definite organization of political and religious thought—a functioning body of philosophers represented in Spain by no less an individual than Cervantes, in France by Cagliostro and St. Germain, in Germany by Gichtel and Andreae, in England by Bacon, More, and Raleigh, and in America by Washington and Franklin. Coincident with the Baconian agitation in England, the *Fama Fraternitatis* and *Confessio Fraternitatis* appeared in Germany, both of these works being contributions to the establishment of a philosophic government upon the earth. One of the outstanding links between the Rosicrucian Mysteries of the Middle Ages and modern Masonry is Elias Ashmole, the historian of the Order of the Garter and the first Englishman to compile the alchemical writings of the English chemists.

The foregoing may seem to be a useless recital of inanities, but its purpose is to impress upon the reader's mind the philosophical and political situation in Europe at the time of the inception of the Masonic order. A philosophic clan, as it were, which had moved across the face of Europe under such names as the "Illuminati" and the "Rosicrucians," had undermined in a subtle manner the entire structure of regal and sacerdotal supremacy. The founders of Freemasonry were all men who were more or less identified with the progressive tendencies of their day. Mystics, philosophers, and alchemists were all bound together with a secret tie and dedicated to the emancipation of humanity from ignorance and oppression. In my research among ancient books and manuscripts, I have pieced together a little story of probabilities which has a direct bearing upon the subject. Long before the establishment of Freemasonry as a fraternity, a group of mystics founded in Europe what was called the "Society of Unknown Philosophers." Prominent among the profound thinkers who formed the membership of this society were the alchemists, who were engaged in transmuting the political and religious "base metal" of Europe into ethical and spiritual "gold"; the Qabbalists who, as investigators of the superior orders of Nature, sought to discover a stable foundation for human government; and lastly the astrologers who, from a study of the procession of the heavenly bodies, hoped to find therein the rational archetype for all mundane procedure. Here and there is to be found a character who contacted this society. By some it is believed that both Martin Luther and also that great mystic, Philip Melanchthon, were connected with it. The first edition of the King James Bible, which was edited by Francis Bacon and prepared under Masonic supervision, bears more Mason's marks than the Cathedral of Strasburg. The same is true respecting the Masonic symbolism found in the first English edition of Josephus' *History of the Jews*.

    For some time, the Society of Unknown Philosophers moved extraneously to the church. Among the fathers of the church, however, were a great number of scholarly and intelligent men who were keenly interested in philosophy and ethics, prominent among them being the Jesuit Father, Athanasius Kircher, who is recognized as one of the great scholars of his day. Both a Rosicrucian and also a member of the Society of Unknown Philosophers, as revealed by the cryptograms in his writings, Kircher was in harmony with this program of philosophic reconstruction. Since learning was largely limited to churchmen, this body of philosophers soon developed an overwhelming preponderance of ecclesiastics in its membership. The original anti-ecclesiastical ideals of the society were thus speedily reduced to an innocuous state and the organization gradually converted into an actual auxiliary of the church. A small portion of the membership, however, ever maintained an aloofness from the literati of the faith, for it represented an unorthodox class—the alchemists, Rosicrucians, Qabbalists, and magicians. This latter group accordingly retired from the outer body of the society that had thus come to be known as the "Order of the Golden and Rose Cross" and whose adepts were elevated to the dignity of Knights of the Golden Stone. Upon the withdrawal of these initiated adepts, a powerful clerical body remained which possessed considerable of the ancient lore but in many instances lacked the "keys" by which this symbolism could be interpreted. As this body continued to increase in temporal power, its philosophical power grew correspondingly less.

The smaller group of adepts that had withdrawn from the order remained inactive apparently, having retired to what they termed the "House of the Holy Spirit," where they were enveloped by certain "mists" impenetrable to the eyes of the profane. Among these reclusive adepts must be included such well-known Rosicrucians as Robert Fludd, Eugenius Philalethes, John Heydon, Michael Maier, and Henri Khunrath. These adepts in their retirement constituted a loosely organized society which, though lacking the solidarity of a definite fraternity, occasionally initiated a candidate and met annually at a specified place. It was the Comte de Chazal, an initiate of this order, who "raised" Dr. Sigismund Bacstrom while the latter was on the Isle of Mauritius. In due time, the original members of the order passed on, after first entrusting their secrets to carefully chosen successors. In the meantime, a group of men in England, under the leadership of such mystics as Ashmole and Fludd, had resolved upon reintroducing the ancient learning and reclassifying philosophy in accordance with Bacon's plan for a world encyclopedia. These men had undertaken to reconstruct ancient Platonic and Gnostic mysticism, but were unable to attain their objective for lack of information. Elias Ashmole may have been a member of the European order of Rosicrucians and as such evidently knew that in various parts of Europe there were isolated individuals who were in possession of the secret doctrine handed down in unbroken line from the ancient Greeks and Egyptians through Boetius, the early Christian Church, and the Arabians.

The efforts of the English group to contact such individuals were evidently successful. Several initiated Rosicrucians were brought from the mainland to England, where they remained for a considerable time designing the symbolism of Freemasonry and incorporating into the rituals of the order the same divine principles and philosophy that had formed the inner doctrine of all great secret societies from the time of the Eleusinia in Greece. In fact, the Eleusinian Mysteries themselves continued in Christendom until the sixth century after Christ, after which they passed into the custody of the Arabians, as attested by the presence of Masonic symbols and figures upon early Mohammedan monuments. The adepts brought over from the Continent to sit in council with the English philosophers were initiates of the Arabian rites and thus through them the Mysteries were ultimately returned to Christendom. Upon completion of the by-laws of the new fraternity, the initiates retired again into Central Europe, leaving a group of disciples to develop the outer organization, which was to function as a sort of screen to conceal the activities of the esoteric order.

Such, in brief, is the story to be pieced together from the fragmentary bits of evidence available. The whole structure of Freemasonry is founded upon the activities of this secret society of Central European adepts; whom the studious Mason will find to be the definite "link" between the modern Craft and the Ancient Wisdom. The outer body of Masonic philosophy was merely the veil of this qabbalistic order whose members were the custodians of the true Arcanum. Does this inner and secret brotherhood of initiates still exist independent of the Freemasonic order? Evidence points to the fact that it does, for these august adepts are the actual preservers of those secret operative processes of the Greeks whereby the illumination and completion of the individual is affected. They are the veritable guardians of the "Lost Word"—the Keepers of the inner Mystery—and the Mason who searches for and discovers them is rewarded beyond all mortal estimation.

Freemasons and Rosicrucians
The Enlightened

In the preface to a book entitled *Long-Livers*, published in 1772, Eugenius Philalethes, the Rosicrucian initiate, thus addresses his Brethren of the Most Ancient and Most Honorable Fraternity of the Free Masons: "Remember that you are the Salt of the Earth, the Light of the World, and the Fire of the Universe. You are living Stones, built up a Spiritual House, who believe and rely on the chief Lapis Angularis which the refractory and disobedient Builders disallowed. You are called from Darkness to Light; you are a chosen Generation, a royal Priesthood. This makes you, my dear Brethren, fit Companions for the greatest Kings; and no wonder, since the King of Kings hath condescended to make you so to himself, compared to whom the mightiest and most haughty Princes of the Earth are but as Worms, and that not so much as we are all Sons of the same One Eternal Father, by whom all Things were made; but inasmuch as we do the Will of his and our Father which is in Heaven. You see now your high Dignity; you see what you are; act accordingly, and show yourselves (what you are) MEN, and walk worthy the high Profession to which you are called, * * *. Remember, then, what the great End we all aim at is: Is it not to be happy *here* and *hereafter*? For they both depend on each other. The Seeds of that eternal Peace and Tranquility and everlasting Repose must be sown in this Life; and he that would glorify and enjoy the Sovereign Good then must learn to do it now, and from contemplating the Creature gradually ascend to adore the Creator."

Of all obstacles to surmount in matters of rationality, the most difficult is that of prejudice. Even the casual observer must realize that the true wealth of Freemasonry lies in its mysticism. The average Masonic scholar, however, is fundamentally opposed to a mystical interpretation of his symbols, for he shares the attitude of the modern mind in its general antipathy towards transcendentalism. A most significant fact, however, is that those Masons who have won signal honors for their contributions to the Craft have been transcendentalists almost without exception. It is quite incredible, moreover, that any initiated Brother, when presented with a copy of *Morals and Dogma* upon the conferment of his fourteenth degree, can read that volume and yet maintain that his order is not identical with the Mystery Schools of the first ages. Much of the writings of Albert Pike are extracted from the books of the French magician, Eliphas Levi, one of the greatest transcendentalists of modern times. Levi was an occultist, a metaphysician, a Platonic philosopher, who by the rituals of magic invoked even the spirit of Apollonius of Tyana, and yet Pike has inserted in his *Morals and Dogma* whole pages, and even chapters, practically verbatim. To Pike the following remarkable tribute was paid by Stirling Kerr, Jr., 33° Deputy for the Inspector-General for the District of Columbia, upon crowning with laurel the bust of Pike in the House of the Temple: "Pike was an oracle greater than that of Delphi. He was Truth's minister and priest. His victories were those of peace. Long may his memory live in the hearts of the Brethren." Affectionately termed "Albertus Magnus" by his admirers, Pike wrote of Hermeticism and alchemy and hinted at the Mysteries of the Temple. Through his zeal and unflagging energy, American Freemasonry was raised from comparative obscurity to become the most powerful organization in the land. Though Pike, a transcendental thinker, was the recipient of every honor that the Freemasonic bodies of the world could confer, the modern Mason is loath to admit that transcendentalism has any place in Freemasonry. This is an attitude filled with embarrassment and inconsistency, for whichever way the Mason turns he is confronted by these inescapable issues of philosophy and the Mysteries. Yet withal he dismisses the entire subject as being more or less a survival of primitive superstitions.

The Mason who would discover the *Lost Word* must remember, however, that in the first ages—every neophyte was a man of profound learning and unimpeachable character, who for the sake of wisdom and virtue had faced death unafraid and had triumphed over those limitations of the flesh which bind most mortals to the sphere of mediocrity. In those days the rituals were not put on by degree teams who handled candidates as though they were perishable commodities, but by priests deeply versed in the lore of their cults. Not one Freemason out of a thousand could have survived the initiations of the pagan rites, for the tests were given in those strenuous days when men were men and death the reward of failure. The neophyte of the Druid Mysteries was set adrift in a small boat to battle with the stormy sea, and unless his knowledge of natural law enabled him to quell the storm as did Jesus upon the Sea of Galilee, he returned no more. In the Egyptian rites of Serapis, it was required of the neophyte that he cross an unbridged chasm in the temple floor. In other words, if unable by magic to sustain himself in the air without visible support, he fell headlong into a volcanic crevice, there to die of heat and suffocation. In one part of the Mithraic rites, the candidate seeking admission to the inner sanctuary was required to pass through a closed door by dematerialization. The philosopher who has authenticated the reality of ordeals such as these no longer entertains the popular error that the performance of "miracles" is confined solely to Biblical characters. "Do you still ask," writes Pike, "if it has its secrets and mysteries? It is certain that something in the Ancient Initiations was regarded as of immense value, by such Intellects as Herodotus, Plutarch, and Cicero. The Magicians of Egypt were able to imitate several of the miracles wrought by Moses; and the Science of the Hierophants of the mysteries produced effects that to the Initiated seemed Mysterious and supernatural." (See: *Legenda for the Twenty-eighth Degree.*)

It becomes self-evident that he who passed successfully through these arduous tests involving both natural and also supernatural hazards was a man apart in his community. Such an initiate was deemed to be more than human, for he had achieved where countless ordinary mortals, having failed, had returned no more. Let us hear the words of Apuleius when admitted into the Temple of Isis, as recorded in *The Metamorphosis, or Golden Ass*: "Then also the priest, all the profane being removed, taking hold of me by the hand, brought me to the penetralia of the temple, clothed in a new linen garment. Perhaps, inquisitive reader, you will very anxiously ask me what was then said and done? I would tell you, if it could be lawfully told; you should know it, if it was lawful for you to hear it. But both ears and the tongue are guilty of rash curiosity. Nevertheless, I will not keep you in suspense with religious desire, nor torment you with long-continued anxiety. Hear, therefore, but believe what is true. *I approached to the confines of death, and having trod on the threshold of Proserpine, I returned from it, being carried through all the elements. At midnight I saw the sun shining with a splendid light; and I manifestly drew near to the Gods beneath, and the Gods above, and proximately adored them.* Behold, I have narrated to you things, of which, though heard, it is nevertheless necessary that you should be ignorant. I will, therefore, only relate that which may be enunciated to the understanding of the profane without a crime."

Kings and princes paid homage to the initiate—the "newborn" man, the favorite of the gods. The initiate had actually entered into the presence of the divine beings. He had "died" and been "raised" again into the radiant sphere of everlasting light. Seekers after wisdom journeyed across great continents to hear his words and his sayings were treasured with the revelations of oracles. It was even esteemed an honor to receive from such a one an inclination of the head, a kindly smile or a gesture of approbation. Disciples gladly paid with their lives for the Master's word of praise and died of a broken heart at his rebuke. On one occasion, Pythagoras became momentarily irritated because of the seeming stupidity of one of his students. The Master's displeasure so preyed upon the mind of the humiliated youth that, drawing a knife from the folds of his garment, he committed suicide. So greatly moved was Pythagoras by the incident that never from that time on was he known to lose patience with any of his followers regardless of the provocation.

With a smile of paternal indulgence the venerable Master, who senses the true dignity of the mystic tie, should gravely incline the minds of the Brethren towards the sublime issues of the Craft. The officer who would serve his lodge most effectively must realize that he is of an order apart from other men, that he is the keeper of an awful secret, that the chair upon which he sits is the seat of immortals, and that if he would be a worthy successor to those Master Masons of other ages, his thoughts must be measured by the profundity of Pythagoras and the lucidity of Plato. Enthroned in the radiant East, the Worshipful Master is the "Light" of his lodge—the representative of the gods, one of that long line of hierophants who, through the blending of their rational powers with the reason of the Ineffable, have been accepted into the Great School. This high priest after an ancient order must realize that those before him are not merely a gathering of properly tested men, but the custodians of an eternal lore, the guardians of a sacred truth, the perpetuators of an ageless wisdom, the consecrated servants of a living God, the wardens of a Supreme Mystery.

A new day is dawning for Freemasonry. From the insufficiency of theology and the hopelessness of materialism, men are turning to seek the God of philosophy. In this new era wherein the old order of things is breaking down and the individual is rising triumphant above the monotony of the masses, there is much work to be accomplished. The "Temple Builder" is needed as never before. A great reconstruction period is at hand; the debris of a fallen culture must be cleared away; the old footings must be found again that a new Temple significant of a new revelation of Law may be raised thereon. This is the peculiar work of the Builder; this is the high duty for which he was called out of the world; this is the noble enterprise for which he was "raised" and given the tools of his Craft. By thus doing his part in the reorganization of society, the workman may earn his "wages" as all good Masons should. A new light is breaking in the East, a more glorious day is at hand. The rule of the philosophic elect—the dream of the ages—will yet be realized and is not far distant. To her loyal sons, Freemasonry sends this clarion call: "Arise ye, the day of labor is at band; the Great Work awaits completion, and the days of man's life are few." Like the singing guildsman of bygone days, the Craft of the Builders marches victoriously down the broad avenues of Time. Their song is of labor and glorious endeavor; their anthem is of toil and industry; they rejoice in their noble destiny, for they are the Builders of cities, the Hewers of worlds, the Master Craftsmen of the universe!

THE HIRAMIC LEGEND
(1928)

WHEN Solomon—the beloved of God, builder of the Everlasting House, and Grand Master of the Lodge of Jerusalem—ascended the throne of his father David he consecrated his life to the erection of a temple to God and a palace for the kings of Israel. David's faithful friend, Hiram, King of Tyre, hearing that a son of David sat upon the throne of Israel, sent messages of congratulation, and offers of assistance to the new ruler. In his *History of the Jews,* Josephus mentions that copies of the letters passing between the two kings were then to be seen both at Jerusalem and at Tyre. Despite Hiram's lack of appreciation for the twenty cities of Galilee which Solomon presented to him upon the completion of the temple, the two monarchs remained the best of friends. Both were famous for their wit and wisdom, and when they exchanged letters each devised puzzling questions to test the mental ingenuity of the other. Solomon made an agreement with Hiram of Tyre promising vast amounts of barley, wheat, corn, wine, and oil as wages for the masons and carpenters from Tyre who were to assist the Jews in the erection of the temple. Hiram also supplied cedars and other fine trees, which were made into rafts and floated down the sea to Joppa, whence they were taken inland by Solomon's workmen to the temple site.

Because of his great love for Solomon, Hiram of Tyre sent also the Grand Master of the Dionysiac Architects, CHiram Abiff, a Widow's Son, who had no equal among the craftsmen of the earth. CHiram is described as being "a Tyrian by birth, but of Israelitish descent," and "a second Bezaleel, honored by his king with the title of Father." *The Freemason's Pocket Companion* (published in 1771) describes CHiram as "the most cunning, skillful and curious workman that ever lived, whose abilities were not confined to building alone, but extended to all kinds of work, whether in gold, silver, brass or iron; whether in linen, tapestry, or embroidery; whether considered as an architect, statuary *[sic]*; founder or designer, separately or together, he equally excelled. From his designs, and under his direction, all the rich and splendid furniture of the Temple and its several appendages were begun, carried on, and finished. Solomon appointed him, in his absence, to fill the chair, as Deputy Grand-Master; and in his presence, Senior Grand-Warden, Master of work, and general overseer of all artists, as well those whom David had formerly procured from Tyre and Sidon, as those Hiram should now send." (Modem Masonic writers differ as to the accuracy of the last sentence.)

Although an immense amount of labor was involved in its construction, Solomon's Temple—in the words of George Oliver—"was only a small building and very inferior in point of size to some of our churches." The number of buildings contiguous to it and the vast treasure of gold and precious stones used in its construction concentrated a great amount of wealth within the temple area. In the midst of the temple stood the Holy of Holies, sometimes called the Oracle. It was an exact cube, each dimension being twenty cubits, and exemplified the influence of Egyptian symbolism. The buildings of the temple group were ornamented with 1,453 columns of Parian marble, magnificently sculptured, and 2,906 pilasters decorated with capitals. There was a broad porch facing the east, and the *sanctum sanctorum* was upon the west. According to tradition, the various buildings and courtyards could hold in all 300,000 persons. Both the Sanctuary and the Holy of Holies were entirely lined with solid gold plates encrusted with jewels.

King Solomon began the building of the temple in the fourth year of his reign on what would be, according to modern calculation, the 21st day of April, and finished it in the eleventh year of his reign on the 23rd day of October. The temple was begun in the 480th year after the children of Israel had passed the Red Sea. Part of the labor of construction included the building of an artificial foundation on the brow of Mount Moriah. The stones for the temple were hoisted from quarries directly beneath Mount Moriah and were trued before being brought to the surface. The brass and golden ornaments for the temple were cast in molds in the clay ground between Succoth and Zeredatha, and the wooden parts were all finished before they reached the temple site. The building was put together, consequently, without sound and without instruments, all its parts fitting exactly "without the hammer of contention, the axe of division, or any tool of mischief."

Anderson's much-discussed *Constitutions of the Free-Masons,* published in London in 1723, and reprinted by Benjamin Franklin in Philadelphia in 1734, thus describes the division of the laborers engaged in the building of the Everlasting House:

"But Dagon's Temple, and the finest structures of Tyre and Sidon, could not be compared with the Eternal God's Temple at Jerusalem, * * * there were employed about it no less than 3,600 Princes, or Master-Masons, to conduct the work according to Solomon's directions, with 80,000 hewers of stone in the mountain, or Fellow Craftsmen, and 70,000 labourers, in all 153,600 besides the levy under Adoniram to work in the mountains of Lebanon by turns with the Sidonians, viz., 30,000, being in all 183,600." Daniel Sickels gives 3,300 overseers, instead of 3,600, and lists the three Grand Masters separately. The same author estimates the cost of the temple at nearly four thousand millions of dollars.

The Masonic legend of the building of Solomon's Temple does not in every particular parallel the Scriptural version, especially in those portions relating to CHiram Abiff. According to the Biblical account, this Master workman returned to his own country; in the Masonic allegory he is foully murdered. On this point A. E. Waite, in his *New Encyclopædia of Freemasonry,* makes the following explanatory comment:

"The legend of the Master-Builder is the great allegory of Masonry. It happens that his figurative story is grounded on the fact of a personality mentioned in Holy Scripture, but this historical background is of the accidents and not the essence; the significance is in the allegory and not in any point of history which may lie behind it."

CHiram, as Master of the Builders, divided his workmen into three groups, which were termed *Entered Apprentices, Fellow-Craftsmen,* and *Master Masons.* To each division he gave certain passwords and signs by which their respective excellence could be quickly determined. While all were classified according to their merits some were dissatisfied, for they desired a more exalted position than they were capable of filling. At last, three Fellow-Craftsmen, more daring than their companions, determined to force CHiram to reveal to them the password of the Master's degree. Knowing that CHiram always went into the unfinished *sanctum sanctorum* at high noon to pray, these *ruffians*—whose names were Jubela, Jubelo, and Jubelum—lay in wait for him, one at each of the main gates of the temple. CHiram, about to leave the temple by the south gate, was suddenly confronted by Jubela armed with a twenty-four-inch gauge. Upon CHiram's refusal to reveal the Master's *Word*, the ruffian struck him on the throat with the rule, and the wounded Master then hastened to the west gate, where Jubelo, armed with a square, awaited him and made a similar demand. Again CHiram was silent, and the second assassin struck him on the breast with the square. CHiram thereupon staggered to the east gate, only to be met there by Jubelum armed with a maul. When CHiram, refused him the Master's Word, Jubelum struck the Master between the eyes with the mallet and CHiram fell dead.

The body of CHiram was buried by the murderers over the brow of Mount Moriah and a sprig of acacia placed upon the grave. The murderers then sought to escape punishment for their crime by embarking for Ethiopia, but the port was closed. All three were finally captured, and after admitting their guilt were duly executed. Parties of three were then sent out by King Solomon, and one of these groups discovered the newly made grave marked by the evergreen sprig. After the Entered Apprentices and the Fellow-Craftsmen had failed to resurrect

The Hiramic Legend

their Master from the dead he was finally *raised* by the Master Mason with the "strong grip of a Lion's Paw."

To the initiated Builder the name *CHiram Abiff* signifies "My Father, the Universal Spirit, one in essence, three in aspect." Thus, the murdered Master is a type of the Cosmic Martyr—the crucified Spirit of Good, the *dying god*—whose Mystery is celebrated throughout the world. Among the manuscripts of Dr. Sigismund Bastrom, the initiated Rosicrucian, appears the following extract from von Welling concerning the true philosophic nature of the Masonic CHiram:

"The original word, *CHiram*, is a radical word consisting of three consonants, *Cheth*, *Resh* and *Mem*. (1) *Cheth*, signifies *Chamah*, the Sun's light, i. e. the *Universal, invisible, cold fire of Nature* attracted by the Sun, manifested into *light* and sent down to us and to every planetary body belonging to the solar system. (2) *Resh*, signifies *Ruach*, i. e. *Spirit, air, wind*, as being the Vehicle which conveys and collects the light into numberless Foci, wherein the solar rays of light are agitated by a circular motion and manifested in *Heat* and *burning Fire*. (3) *Mem*, signifies *majim, water, humidity*, but rather the *mother of water*, i. e. Radical Humidity or a particular kind of condensed air. These three constitute the Universal Agent or fire of Nature in one word, *CHiram*, not *Hiram*."

Albert Pike mentions several forms of the name *CHiram: Khirm, Khurm*, and *Khur-Om*, the latter ending in the sacred Hindu monosyllable *OM*, which may also be extracted from the names of the three murderers. Pike further relates the three ruffians to a triad of stars in the constellation of Libra and also calls attention to the fact that the Chaldean god Bal—metamorphosed into a demon by the Jews—appears in the name of each of the murderers, Ju*bel*a, Ju*bel*o, and Ju*bel*um. To interpret the Hiramic legend requires familiarity with both the Pythagorean and Qabbalistic systems of numbers and letters, and also the philosophic and astronomic cycles of the Egyptians, Chaldeans, and Brahmins. For example, consider the number 33. The first temple of Solomon stood for thirty-three years in its pristine splendor. At the end of that time it was pillaged by the Egyptian King Shishak, and finally (588 B.C.) it was completely destroyed by Nebuchadnezzar and the people of Jerusalem were led into captivity to Babylon. (See *General History of Freemasonry*, by Robert Macoy.) Also, King David ruled for thirty-three years in Jerusalem; the Masonic Order is divided into thirty-three symbolic degrees; there are thirty-three segments in the human spinal column; and Jesus was crucified in the thirty-third year of His life.

The efforts made to discover the origin of the Hiramic legend show that, while the legend in its present form is comparatively modem, its underlying principles run back to remotest antiquity. It is generally admitted by modern Masonic scholars that the story of the martyred CHiram is based upon the Egyptian rites of Osiris, whose death and resurrection figuratively portrayed the spiritual death of man and his regeneration through initiation into the Mysteries. CHiram is also identified with Hermes through the inscription on the Emerald Table. From these associations it is evident that CHiram is to be considered as a prototype of humanity; in fact, he is Plato's *Idea* (archetype) of man. As Adam after the Fall symbolizes the Idea of human degeneration, so CHiram through his resurrection symbolizes the Idea of human regeneration.

On the 19th day of March, 1314, Jacques de Molay, the last Grand Master of the Knights Templars, was burned on a pyre erected upon that point of the islet of the Seine, at Paris, where afterwards was erected the statue of King Henry IV. (See *The Indian Religions*, by Hargrave Jennings.) "It is mentioned as a tradition in some of the accounts of the burning," writes Jennings, "that Molay, ere he expired, summoned Clement, the Pope who had pronounced the bull of abolition against the Order and had condemned the Grand Master to the flames, to appear, within forty days, before the Supreme Eternal judge, and Philip [the king] to the same awful tribunal within the space of a year. Both predictions were fulfilled." The close relationship between Freemasonry and the original Knights Templars has caused the story of CHiram to be linked with the martyrdom of Jacques de

Molay. According to this interpretation, the three *ruffians* who cruelly slew their Master at the gates of the temple because he refused to reveal the secrets of his Order represent the Pope, the king, and the executioners. De Molay died maintaining his innocence and refusing to disclose the philosophical and magical arcana of the Templars.

Those who have sought to identify CHiram with the murdered King Charles the First conceive the Hiramic legend to have been invented for that purpose by Elias Ashmole, a mystical philosopher, who was probably a member of the Rosicrucian Fraternity. Charles was dethroned in 1647 and died on the block in 1649, leaving the Royalist party leaderless. An attempt has been made to relate the term "the Sons of the Widow" (an appellation frequently applied to members of the Masonic Order) to this incident in English history, for by the murder of her king England became a *Widow* and all Englishmen *Widow's Sons*.

To the mystic Christian Mason, CHiram. represents the Christ who in three days (degrees) *raised* the temple of His body from its earthly sepulcher. His three murderers were Cæsar's agent (the state), the Sanhedrin (the church), and the incited populace (the mob). Thus considered, CHiram becomes the higher nature of man, and the murderers are ignorance, superstition, and fear. The indwelling Christ can give expression to Himself in this world only through man's thoughts, feelings, and actions. Right thinking, right feeling, and right action—these are three gates through which the Christ power passes into the material world, there to labor in the erection of the Temple of Universal Brotherhood. Ignorance, superstition, and fear are three ruffians through whose agencies the Spirit of Good is murdered and a false kingdom, controlled by wrong thinking, wrong feeling, and wrong action, established in its stead. In the material universe evil appears ever victorious.

"In this sense," writes Daniel Sickels, "the myth of the Tyrian is perpetually repeated in the history of human affairs. Orpheus was murdered, and his body thrown into the Hebrus; Socrates was made to drink the hemlock; and, in all ages, we have seen Evil temporarily triumphant, and Virtue and Truth calumniated, persecuted, crucified, and slain. But Eternal justice marches surely and swiftly through the world: the Typhons, the children of darkness, the plotters of crime, all the infinitely varied forms of evil, are swept into oblivion; and Truth and Virtue—for a time laid low—come forth, clothed with diviner majesty, and crowned with everlasting glory!" (See *General Ahiman Rezon.*)

If, as there is ample reason to suspect, the modern Freemasonic Order was profoundly influenced by, if it is not an actual outgrowth of, Francis Bacon's secret society, its symbolism is undoubtedly permeated with Bacon's two great ideals: universal education and universal democracy. The deadly enemies of universal education are ignorance, superstition, and fear, by which the human soul is held in bondage to the lowest part of its own constitution. The arrant enemies of universal democracy have ever been the crown, the tiara, and the torch. Thus CHiram symbolizes that ideal state of spiritual, intellectual, and physical emancipation which has ever been sacrificed upon the altar of human selfishness. CHiram is the Beautifier of the Eternal House. Modern utilitarianism, however, sacrifices the beautiful for the practical, in the same breath declaring the obvious lie that selfishness, hatred, and discord are practical.

Dr. Orville Ward Owen found a considerable part of the first thirty-two degrees of Freemasonic ritualism hidden in the text of the First Shakespeare Folio. Masonic emblems are to be observed also upon the title pages of nearly every book published by Bacon. Sir Francis Bacon considered himself as a living sacrifice upon the altar of human need; he was obviously *cut down* in the midst of his labors, and no student of his *New Atlantis* can fail to recognize the Masonic symbolism contained therein. According to the observations of Joseph Fort Newton, the Temple of Solomon described by Bacon in that utopian romance was not a house at all but the name of an ideal state. Is it not true that the Temple of Freemasonry is also emblematic of a condition of society? While, as before stated, the principles of the Hiramic legend are of the greatest antiquity, it is not impossible that its present form may be based upon incidents in

The Hiramic Legend

the life of Lord Bacon, who passed through the philosophic death and was *raised* in Germany.

In an old manuscript appears the statement that the Freemasonic Order was formed by alchemists and Hermetic philosophers who had banded themselves together to protect their secrets against the infamous methods used by avaricious persons to wring from them the secret of gold-making. The fact that the Hiramic legend contains an alchemical formula gives credence to this story. Thus the building of Solomon's Temple represents the consummation of the *magnum opus*, which cannot be realized without the assistance of CHiram, the Universal Agent. The Masonic Mysteries teach the initiate how to prepare within his own soul a miraculous *powder of projection* by which it is possible for him to transmute the base lump of human ignorance, perversion, and discord into an ingot of spiritual and philosophic gold.

Sufficient similarity exists between the Masonic CHiram and the *Kundalini* of Hindu mysticism to warrant the assumption that CHiram may be considered a symbol also of the Spirit Fire moving through the sixth ventricle of the spinal column. The exact science of human regeneration is the Lost Key of Masonry, for when the Spirit Fire is *lifted up* through the thirty-three degrees, or segments of the spinal column, and enters into the domed chamber of the human skull, it finally passes into the pituitary body (Isis), where it invokes Ra (the pineal gland) and demands the Sacred Name. Operative Masonry, in the fullest meaning of that term, signifies the process by which the Eye of Horus is opened. E. A. Wallis Budge has noted that in some of the papyri illustrating the entrance of the souls of the dead into the judgment hall of Osiris the deceased person has a pinecone attached to the crown of his head. The Greek mystics also carried a symbolic staff, the upper end being in the form of a pinecone, which was called the *thyrsus* of Bacchus. In the human brain there is a tiny gland called the pineal body, which is the sacred eye of the ancients, and corresponds to the third eye of the Cyclops. Little is known concerning the function of the pineal body, which Descartes suggested (more wisely than he knew) might be the abode of the spirit of man. As its name signifies, the pineal gland is the sacred pinecone in man—the *eye single*, which cannot be opened until CHiram (the Spirit Fire) is *raised* through the sacred seals which are called the Seven Churches in Asia.

There is an Oriental painting which shows three sun bursts. One sunburst covers the head, in the midst of which sits Brahma with four heads, his body a mysterious dark color. The second sunburst—which covers the heart, solar plexus, and upper abdominal region—shows Vishnu sitting in the blossom of the lotus on a couch formed of the coils of the serpent of cosmic motion, its seven-hooded head forming a canopy over the god. The third sunburst is over the generative system, in the midst of which sits Shiva, his body a grayish white and the Ganges River flowing out of the crown of his head. This painting was the work of a Hindu mystic who spent many years subtly concealing great philosophical principles within these figures. The Christian legends could be related also to the human body by the same method as the Oriental, for the arcane meanings hidden in the teachings of both schools are identical.

As applied to Masonry, the three sunbursts represent the gates of the temple at which CHiram was struck, there being no gate in the north because the sun never shines from the northern angle of the heavens. The north is the symbol of the physical because of its relation to ice (crystallized water) and to the body (crystallized spirit). In man the light shines toward the north but never from it, because the body has no light of its own but shines with the reflected glory of the divine life-particles concealed within physical substance. For this reason, the moon is accepted as the symbol of man's physical nature. CHiram is the mysterious fiery, airy water which must be raised through the three grand centers symbolized by the ladder with three rungs and the sunburst flowers mentioned in the description of the Hindu painting. It must also pass upward by means of the ladder of seven rungs—the seven plexuses proximate to the spine. The nine segments of the sacrum and coccyx are pierced by ten foramina, through which pass the roots of the Tree of Life. Nine is the sacred number of man, and in the symbolism of the sacrum and coccyx a great mystery is concealed. That part of the body from the kidneys downward was termed by the early Qabbalists the *Land of Egypt* into which the children of Israel were taken during the captivity. Out of Egypt, Moses (the illuminated mind, as his name implies) led the tribes of Israel (the twelve faculties) by *raising* the brazen serpent in the wilderness upon the symbol of the Tau cross. Not only CHiram but the god-men of nearly every pagan Mystery ritual are personifications of the Spirit Fire in the human spinal cord.

The astronomical aspect of the Hiramic legend must not be overlooked. The tragedy of CHiram is enacted annually by the sun during its passage through the signs of the zodiac.

"From the journey of the Sun through the twelve signs," writes Albert Pike, "come the legend of the twelve labors of Hercules, and the incarnations of Vishnu and Buddha. Hence came the legend of the murder of Khurum, representative of the Sun, by the three Fellow-Crafts, symbols of the Winter signs, Capricornus, Aquarius, and Pisces, who assailed him at the three gates of Heaven and slew him at the Winter Solstice. Hence the search for him by the nine Fellow-Crafts, the other nine signs, his finding, burial, and resurrection." (See *Morals and Dogma.)*

Other authors consider Libra, Scorpio, and Sagittarius as the three murderers of the sun, inasmuch as Osiris was murdered by Typhon, to whom were assigned the thirty degrees of the constellation of Scorpio. In the Christian Mysteries also Judas signifies the Scorpion, and the thirty pieces of silver for which he betrayed His Lord represent the number of degrees in that sign. Having been struck by Libra (the state), Scorpio (the church), and Sagittarius (the mob), the sun (CHiram) is secretly home through the darkness by the signs of Capricorn, Aquarius, and Pisces and buried over the brow of a hill (the vernal equinox). Capricorn has for its symbol an old man with a scythe in his hand. This is Father Time—a wayfarer—who is symbolized in Masonry as straightening out the ringlets of a young girl's hair. If the Weeping Virgin be considered a symbol of Virgo, and Father Time with his scythe a symbol of Capricorn, then the interval of ninety degrees between these two signs will be found to correspond to that occupied by the three murderers. Esoterically, the urn containing the ashes of CHiram represents the human heart. Saturn, the old man who lives at the north pole, and brings with him to the children of men a sprig of evergreen (the Christmas tree), is familiar to the little folks under the name of *Santa Claus,* for he brings each winter the gift of a new year.

The martyred sun is discovered by Aries, a Fellow-Craftsman, and at the vernal equinox the process of raising him begins. This is finally accomplished by the Lion of Judah, who in ancient times occupied the position of the keystone of the Royal Arch of Heaven. The precession of the equinoxes causes various signs to play the role of the murderers of the sun during the different ages of the world, but the principle involved remains unchanged. Such is the cosmic story of CHiram, the Universal Benefactor, the Fiery Architect: of the Divine House, who carries with him to the grave that Lost Word which, when spoken, *raises* all life to power and glory. According to Christian mysticism, when the Lost Word is found it is discovered in a stable, surrounded by beasts and marked by a star. "After the sun leaves Leo," writes Robert Hewitt Brown, "the days begin to grow unequivocally shorter as the sun declines toward the autumnal equinox, to be again slain by the *three* autumnal months, lie dead through the *three* winter ones, and be raised again by the *three* vernal ones. Each year the great tragedy is repeated, and the glorious resurrection takes place." (See *Stellar Theology and Masonic Astronomy.)*

CHiram is termed *dead* because in the average individual the cosmic creative forces are limited in their manifestation to purely physical—and correspondingly materialistic—expression. Obsessed by his belief in the reality and permanence of physical existence, man does not correlate the material universe with the blank north wall of the temple. As the solar light symbolically is said to die as it approaches the winter solstice, so the physical world may be termed to the mythological *fall* of man, at which time the human spirit descended into the realms of Hades by being immersed in the illusion of terrestrial existence.

In *An Essay on the Beautiful,* Plotinus describes the refining effect of beauty upon the unfolding consciousness of man. Commissioned to decorate the Everlasting House, CHiram Abiff is the embodiment of the beautifying principle. Beauty is essential to the natural unfoldment of the human soul. The Mysteries held that man, in part at least, was the product of his environment. Therefore, they considered it imperative that every person be surrounded by objects which would evoke the highest and noblest sentiments. They proved that it was possible to produce beauty in life by surrounding life with beauty. They discovered that symmetrical bodies were built by souls continuously in the presence of symmetrical bodies; that noble thoughts were produced by minds surrounded by examples of mental nobility. Conversely, if a man were forced to look upon an ignoble or asymmetrical structure it would arouse within him a sense of ignobility which would provoke him to commit ignoble deeds. If an ill-proportioned building were erected in the midst of a city there would be ill-proportioned children born in that community; and men and women, gazing upon the asymmetrical structure, would live inharmonious lives. Thoughtful men of antiquity realized that their great philosophers were the natural products of the æsthetic ideals of architecture, music, and art established as the standards of the cultural systems of the time.

The substitution of the discord of the fantastic for the harmony of the beautiful constitutes one of the great tragedies of every civilization. Not only were the Savior-Gods of the ancient world beautiful, but each performed a ministry of beauty, seeking to effect man's regeneration by arousing within him the love of the beautiful. A renaissance of the golden age of fable can be made possible only by the elevation of beauty to its rightful dignity as the all-pervading, idealizing quality in the religious, ethical, sociological, scientific, and political departments of life. The Dionysiac Architects were consecrated to the *raising* of their Master Spirit—Cosmic Beauty—from the sepulcher of material ignorance and selfishness by erecting buildings which were such perfect exemplars of symmetry and majesty that they were actually magical formula by which was evoked the spirit of the martyred Beautifier entombed within a materialistic world.

In the Masonic Mysteries the triune spirit of man (the light Delta) is symbolized by the three Grand Masters of the Lodge of Jerusalem. As God is the pervading principle of three worlds, in each of which He manifests as an active principle, so the spirit of man, partaking of the nature of Divinity, dwells upon three planes of being: the Supreme, the Superior, and the Inferior spheres of the Pythagoreans. At the gate of the Inferior sphere (the underworld, or dwelling place of mortal creatures) stands the guardian of Hades—the three—headed dog Cerberus, who is analogous to the three murderers of the Hiramic legend. According to this symbolic interpretation of the triune spirit, CHiram is the third, or incarnating, part—the Master Builder who through all ages erects living temples of flesh and blood as shrines of the Most High. CHiram comes forth as a flower and is cut down; he *dies* at the gates of matter; he is *buried* in the elements of creation, but—like Thor—he swings his mighty hammer in the fields of space, sets the primordial atoms in motion, and establishes order out of Chaos. As the potentiality of cosmic power within each human soul, CHiram lies waiting for man by the elaborate ritualism of life to transmute potentiality into divine potency. As the sense perceptions of the individual increase, however, man gains ever greater control over his various parts, and the spirit of life within gradually attains freedom. The three murderers represent the laws of the Inferior world—birth, growth, and decay—which ever frustrate the plan of the Builder. To the average individual, physical birch actually signifies the death of CHiram, and physical death the resurrection of CHiram. To the initiate, however, the resurrection of the spiritual nature is accomplished without the intervention of physical death.

The curious symbols found in the base of Cleopatra's Needle now standing in Central Park, New York, were interpreted as being of first Masonic significance by S. A. Zola, 33° Past Grand Master of the Grand Lodge of Egypt. Masons' marks and symbols are to be found on the stones of numerous public buildings not only in England and on the Continent but also in Asia. In his *Indian Masons' Marks of the Moghul Dynasty*, A. Gorham describes scores of markings appearing on the walls of buildings such as the *Taj Mahal*, the *Jama Masjid*, and that: famous Masonic structure, the *Kutab Minar*. According to those who regard Masonry as an outgrowth of the secret society of architects and builders which for thousands of years formed a caste of master craftsmen, CHiram Abiff was the Tyrian Grand Master of a world-wide organization of artisans, with headquarters in Tyre. Their philosophy consisted of incorporating into the measurements and ornamentation of temples, palaces, mausoleums, fortresses, and other public buildings their knowledge of the laws controlling the universe. Every initiated workman was given a hieroglyphic with which he marked the stones he trued to show to all posterity that he thus dedicated to the Supreme Architect of the Universe each perfected product of his labor. Concerning Masons' marks, Robert Freke Gould writes:

"It is very remarkable that these marks are to be found in all countries—in the chambers of the Great Pyramid at Gizeh, on the underground walls of Jerusalem, in Herculaneum and Pompeii, on Roman walls and Grecian temples, in Hindustan, Mexico, Peru, Asia Minor—as well as on the great ruins of England, France, Germany, Scotland, Italy, Portugal and Spain." (See *A Concise History of Freemasonry*.)

From this viewpoint the story of CHiram may well represent the incorporation of the divine secrets of architecture into the actual parts and dimensions of earthly buildings. The three degrees of the Craft bury the Grand Master (the Great Arcanum) in the actual structure they erect, after first having *killed* him with the builders' tools, by reducing the dimensionless Spirit of Cosmic Beauty to the limitations of concrete form. These abstract ideals of architecture can be resurrected, however, by the Master Mason who, by meditating upon the structure, releases therefrom the divine principles of architectonic philosophy incorporated or *buried* within it. Thus, the physical building is actually the tomb or embodiment of the Creative Ideal of which its material dimensions are but the shadow.

Moreover, the Hiramic legend may be considered to embody the vicissitudes of philosophy itself. As institutions for the dissemination of ethical culture, the pagan Mysteries were the architects of civilization. Their power and dignity were personified in CHiram Abiff—the Master Builder—but they eventually fell a victim to the onslaughts of that recurrent trio of state, church, and mob. They were desecrated by the state, jealous of their wealth and power; by the early church, fearful of their wisdom; and by the rabble or soldiery incited by both state and church. As CHiram when *raised* from his grave whispers the Master Mason's Word which was lost through his untimely death, so according to the tenets of philosophy the reestablishment or resurrection of the ancient Mysteries will result in the rediscovery of that secret teaching without which civilization must continue in a state of spiritual confusion and uncertainty.

When the mob governs, man is ruled by ignorance; when the church governs, he is ruled by superstition; and when the state governs, he is ruled by fear. Before men can live together in harmony and understanding, ignorance must be transmuted into wisdom, superstition into an illumined faith, and fear into love. Despite statements to the contrary, Masonry is a religion seeking to unite God and man by elevating its initiates to that level of consciousness whereon they can behold with clarified vision the workings of the Great Architect of the Universe. From age to age the vision of a perfect civilization is preserved as the ideal for mankind. In the midst of that civilization shall stand a mighty university wherein both the sacred and secular sciences concerning the mysteries of life will be freely taught to all who will assume the philosophic life. Here creed and dogma will have no place; the superficial will be removed and only the essential be preserved. The world will be ruled by its most illumined minds, and each will occupy the position for which he is most admirably fitted.

The great university will be divided into grades, admission to which will be through preliminary tests or initiations. Here mankind will be instructed in the most sacred, the most secret, and the most enduring of all Mysteries—*Symbolism.* Here the initiate will be taught that every visible object, every abstract thought, every emotional reaction is but the symbol of an eternal principle. Here mankind will learn that CHiram (Truth) lies buried in every atom of Kosmos; that every form is a symbol and every symbol the tomb of an eternal verity. Through education—spiritual, mental, moral, and physical—man will learn to release living truths from their lifeless coverings. The perfect government of the earth must be patterned eventually after that divine government by which the universe is ordered. In that day when perfect order is reestablished, with peace universal and good triumphant, men will no longer seek for happiness, for they shall find it welling up within themselves. Dead hopes, dead aspirations, dead virtues shall rise from their graves, and the Spirit of Beauty and Goodness repeatedly slain by ignorant men shall again be the Master of Work. Then shall sages sit upon the seats of the mighty and the gods walk with men.

*Freemasons and Rosicrucians
The Enlightened*

The Lost Keys of Freemasonry
(1923)

Introduction

FREEMASONRY, though not a religion, is essentially religious. Most of its legends and allegories are of a sacred nature; much of it is woven into the structure of Christianity. We have learned to consider our own religion as the only inspired one, and this probably accounts for much of the misunderstanding in the world today concerning the place occupied by Freemasonry in the spiritual ethics of our race. A religion is a divinely inspired code of morals. A religious person is one inspired to nobler living by this code. He is identified by the code which is his source of illumination. Thus we may say that a Christian is one who receives his spiritual ideals of right and wrong from the message of the Christ, while a Buddhist is one who molds his life into the archetype of morality given by the great Gautama, or one of the other Buddhas. All doctrines which seek to unfold and preserve that invisible spark in man named Spirit, are said to be spiritual. Those which ignore this invisible element and concentrate entirely upon the visible are said to be material. There is in religion a wonderful point of balance, where the materialist and spiritist meet on the plane of logic and reason.

Science and theology are two ends of a single truth, but the world will never receive the full benefit of their investigations until they have made peace with each other, and labor hand in hand for the accomplishment of the great work — the liberation of spirit and intelligence from the three-dimensional prison-house of ignorance, superstition, and fear. That which gives man a knowledge of himself can be inspired only by the Self — and God is the Self in all things. In truth, He is the inspiration and the thing inspired. It has been stated in Scripture that God was the Word and that the Word was made flesh. Man's task now is to make flesh reflect the glory of that Word, which is within the soul of himself. It is this task which has created the need of religion – not one faith alone but many creeds, each searching in its own way, each meeting the needs of individual people, each emphasizing one point above all the others.

Twelve Fellow Craftsmen are exploring the four points of the compass. Are not these twelve the twelve great world religions, each seeking in its own way for that which was lost in the ages past, and the quest of which is the birthright of man? Is not the quest for Reality in a world of illusions the task for which each comes into the world? We are here to gain balance in a sphere of unbalance; to find rest in a restless thing; to unveil illusion; and to slay the dragon of our own animal natures. As David, King of Israel, gave to the hands of his son Solomon the task he could not accomplish, so each generation gives to the next the work of building the temple, or rather, rebuilding the dwelling of the Lord, which is on Mount Moriah.

Truth is not lost, yet it must be sought for and found. Reality is ever-present — dimensionless yet all-prevailing. Man — creature of attitudes and desires, and servant of impressions and opinions — cannot, with the wavering unbalance of an untutored mind, learn to know that which he himself does not possess. As man attains a quality, he discovers that quality, and recognizes about him the thing newborn within himself. Man is born with eyes, yet only after long years of sorrow does he learn to see clearly and in harmony with the Plan. He is born with senses, but only after long experience and fruitless strivings does he bring these senses to the temple and lays them as offerings upon the altar of the great Father, who alone does all things well and with understanding. Man is, in truth, born in the sin of ignorance, but with a capacity for understanding. He has a mind capable of wisdom, a heart capable of feeling, and a hand strong for the great work in life — truing the rough ashlar into the perfect stone.

What more can any creature ask than the opportunity to prove the thing he is, the dream that inspires him, the vision that leads him on? We have no right to ask for wisdom. In whose name do we beg for understanding? By what authority do we demand happiness? None of these things is the birthright of any creature; yet all may have them, if they will cultivate within themselves the thing that they desire. There is no need of asking, nor does any Deity bow down to give man these things that he desires. Man is given by Nature, a gift, and that gift is the privilege of labor. Through labor he learns all things.

Religions are groups of people, gathered together in the labor of learning. The world is a school. We are here to learn, and our presence here proves our need of instruction. Every living creature is struggling to break the strangling bonds of limitation — that pressing narrowness which inhabits vision and leaves the life without an ideal. Every soul is engaged in a great work — the labor of personal liberation from the state of ignorance. The world is a great prison; its bars are the Unknown. And each is a prisoner until, at last, he earns the right to tear these bars from their moldering sockets, and pass, illuminated and inspired, into the darkness, which becomes lighted by that presence. All peoples seek the temple where God dwells, where the spirit of the great Truth illuminates the shadows of human ignorance, but they know not which way to turn nor where this temple is. The mist of dogma surrounds them. Ages of thoughtlessness bind them in. Limitation weakens them and retards their footsteps. They wander in darkness seeking light, failing to realize that the light is in the heart of the darkness.

To the few who have found Him, God is revealed. These, in turn, reveal Him to man, striving to tell ignorance the message of wisdom. But seldom does man understand the mystery that has been unveiled. He tries weakly to follow in the steps of those who have attained, but all too often finds the path more difficult than he even dreamed. So he kneels in prayer before the mountain he cannot climb, from whose top gleams the light which he is neither strong enough to reach nor wise enough to comprehend. He lives the law as he knows it, always fearing in his heart that he has not read aright the flaming letters in the sky, and that in living the letter of the Law he has murdered the spirit. Man bows humbly to the Unknown, peopling the shadows of his own ignorance with saints and saviors, ghosts and specters, gods, and demons. Ignorance fears all things, falling, terror-stricken before the passing wind. Superstition stands as the monument to ignorance, and before it kneels all who realize their own weakness; who see in all things the strength they do not possess; who give to sticks and stones the power to bruise them; who change the beauties of Nature into the dwelling place of ghouls and ogres. Wisdom fears nothing, but still bows humbly to its own Source. While superstition hates all things, wisdom, with its deeper understanding, loves all things; for it has seen the beauty, the tenderness, and the sweetness which underlie Life's mystery.

Life is the span of time appointed for accomplishment. Every fleeting moment is an opportunity, and those who are great are the ones who have recognized life as the opportunity for all things. Arts, sciences, and religions are monuments standing for what humanity has already accomplished. They stand as memorials to the unfolding mind of man, and through them man acquires more efficient and more intelligent methods of attaining prescribed results. Blessed are those who can profit by the experiences of others; who, adding to that which has already been built, can make their inspiration real, their dreams practical. Those who give man the things he needs, while seldom appreciated in their own age, are later recognized as the Saviors of the human race. Masonry is a structure built upon experience. Each stone is a sequential step in the unfolding of intelligence. The shrines of Masonry are ornamented by the jewels of a thousand ages; its rituals ring with the words of enlightened seers and illuminated sages. A hundred religions have brought their gifts of wisdom to its altar. Arts and sciences unnumbered have contributed to its symbolism. It is more than a faith; it is a path of certainty. It is more than a belief; it is a fact. Masonry is a university, teaching the liberal arts and sciences of the soul to all who will attend to its words. It is a shadow of the great Atlantean Mystery School, which stood with all its splendor in the ancient City of the Golden Gates, where now the turbulent Atlantic rolls in unbroken sweep. Its chairs are seats of learning; its pillars uphold the arch of universal education, not only in material things, but also in those qualities which are of the spirit. Up on its trestleboards are inscribed the sacred truths of all nations and of all peoples, and upon those who understand its sacred depths has dawned the great Reality. Masonry is, in truth, that long-lost thing which all peoples have sought in all ages. Masonry is the common denominator as well as the common devisor of human aspiration.

Most of the religions of the world are like processions: one leads, and the many follow. In the footsteps of the demigods, man follows in his search for truth and illumination. The Christian follows the gentle Nazarene up the winding slopes of Calvary. The Buddhist follows his great emancipator through his wanderings in the wilderness. The Mohammedan makes his pilgrimage across the desert sands to the black tent at Mecca. Truth leads, and ignorance follows in his train. Spirit blazes the trail, and matter follows behind. In the world today ideals live but a moment in their purity, before the gathering hosts of darkness snuff out the gleaming spark. The Mystery School, however, remains unmoved. It does not bring its light to man; man must bring his light to it. Ideals, coming into the world, become idols within a few short hours, but man, entering the gates of the sanctuary, changes the idol back to an ideal.

Man is climbing an endless flight of steps, with his eyes fixed upon the goal at the top. Many cannot see the goal, and only one or two steps are visible before them. He has learned, however, one great lesson — namely, that as he builds his own character, he is given strength to climb the steps. Hence a Mason is a builder of the temple of character. He is the architect of a sublime mystery — the gleaming, glowing temple of his own soul. He realizes that he best serves God when he joins with the Great Architect in building more noble structures in the universe below. All who are attempting to attain mastery through constructive efforts are Masons at heart, regardless of religious sect or belief. A Mason is not necessarily a member of a lodge. In a broad sense, he is any person who daily tries to live the Masonic life, and to serve intelligently the needs of the Great Architect. The Masonic brother pledges himself to assist all other temple-builders in whatever extremity of life; and in so doing he pledges himself to every living thing, for they are all temple-builders, building more noble structures to the glory of the universal God.

The true Masonic Lodge is a Mystery School, a place where candidates are taken out of the follies and foibles of the world and instructed in the mysteries of life, relationships, and the identity of that germ of spiritual essence within, which is, in truth, the Son of God, beloved of His Father. The Mason views life seriously, realizing that every wasted moment is a lost opportunity, and that Omnipotence is gained only through earnestness and endeavor. Above all other relationships he recognizes the universal brotherhood of every living thing. The symbol of the clasped hands, explained in the Lodge, reflects his attitude towards all the world, for he is the comrade of all created things. He realizes also that his spirit is a glowing, gleaming jewel which he must enshrine within a holy temple built by the labor of his hands, the meditation of his heart, and the aspiration of his soul. Freemasonry is a philosophy which is essentially creedless. It is the truer for it. Its brothers bow to truth regardless of the bearer; they serve light, instead of wrangling over the one who brings it. In this way they prove that they are seeking to know better the will and the dictates of the Invincible One. No truer religion exists than that of world comradeship and brotherhood, for the purpose of glorifying one God and building for Him a temple of constructive attitude and noble character.

Prologue
In the Fields of Chaos

The first flush of awakening Life pierced the impenetrable expanse of Cosmic Night, turning the darkness of negation into the dim twilight of unfolding being. Silhouetted against the shadowy gateways of Eternity, the lonely figure of a mystic stranger stood upon the nebulous banks of swirling substance. Robed in a shimmery blue mantle of mystery and his head encircled by a golden crown of dazzling light, the darkness of Chaos fled before the rays that poured like streams of living fire from his form divine. From some Cosmos greater far than ours this mystic visitor came, answering the call of Divinity. From star to star he strode and from world to universe he was known, yet forever concealed by the filmy garments of chaotic night. Suddenly the clouds broke and a wondrous light descended from somewhere among the seething waves of force; it bathed this lonely form in a radiance celestial, each sparkling crystal of mist gleaming like a diamond bathed in the living fire of the Divine.

In the gleaming flame of cosmic light bordered by the dark clouds of not — being two great forms appeared and a mighty Voice thrilled eternity, each sparkling atom pulsating with the power of the Creator's Word while the great, blue-robed figure bowed in awe before the foot-stool of His Maker as a hand reached down from heaven, its fingers extended the benediction.

"Of all creation I have chosen you and upon you my seal is placed. You are the chosen instrument of my hand and I appoint you to be the Builder of my Temple. You shall raise its pillars and tile its floor; you shall ornament it with metals and with jewels and you shall be the master of my workmen. In your hands I place the plans and here on the tracing board of living substance I have impressed the plan you are to follow, tracing its every letter and angle in the fiery lines of my moving finger. Hiram Abiff, chosen builder of your Father's house, up and to your work. Yonder are the fleecy clouds, the gray mists of dawn, the gleams of heavenly light, and the darkness of the sleep of creation. From these shall you build, without the sound of hammer or the voice of workmen, the temple of your God, eternal in the heavens.

The swirling, ceaseless motion of negation you shall chain to grind your stones. Among these spirits of not-being shall you slack your lime and lay your footings; for I have watched you through the years of your youth; I have guided you through the days of your manhood. I have weighed you in the balance and you have not been found wanting. Therefore, to you give I the glory of work, and here ordain you as the Builder of my House. Unto you I give the word of the Master Builder; unto you I give the tools of the craft; unto you I give the power that has been vested in me. Be faithful unto these things. Bring them back when you have finished, and I will give you the name known to God alone. So mote it be."

The great light died out of the heavens, the streaming fingers of living light vanished in the misty, lonely twilight, and again covered not-being with its sable mantle. Hiram Abiff again stood alone, gazing out into the endless ocean of oblivion — nothing but swirling, seething matter as far as eye could see. Then he straightened his shoulders and, taking the trestleboard in his hands and clasping to his heart the glowing Word of the Master, walked slowly away, and was swallowed up in the mists of primordial dawn.

How may man measure timeless eternity? Ages passed, and the lonely Builder labored with his plan with only love and humility in his heart, his hand molding the darkness which he blessed while his eyes were raised above where the Great Light had shone down from heaven. In the divine solitude he labored, with no voice to cheer, no spirit to condemn — alone in the boundless all with the great chill of the morning mist upon his brow, but his heart still warm with the light of the Master's Word. It seemed a hopeless task. No single pair of hands could mold that darkness; no single heart, no matter how true, could be great enough to project pulsing cosmic love into the cold mist of oblivion. Though the darkness settled ever closer about him, and the misty fingers of negation twined round his being, still with divine trust the Builder labored; with divine hope he laid his footings, and from the boundless clay he made the molds to cast his sacred ornaments. Slowly the building grew, and dim forms molded by the Master's hand took shape about him. Three huge, soulless creatures had the Master fashioned, great beings which loomed like grim specters in the semi-darkness. They were three builders he had blessed and now in stately file they passed before him, and Hiram held out his arms to his creation, saying, "Brothers, I have built you for your works. I have formed you to labor with me in the building of the Master's house. You are the children of my being; I have labored with you, now labor with me for the glory of our God."

But the specters laughed. Turning upon their maker and striking him with his own tools given him by God out of heaven, they left their Grand Master dying in the midst of his labors, broken and crushed by the threefold powers of cosmic night. As he lay bleeding at the feet of his handiwork the martyred Builder raised his eyes to the seething clouds, and his face was sweet with divine love and cosmic understanding as he prayed unto the Master who had sent him forth:

"O Master of Workmen, Great Architect of the universe, my labors are not finished. Why must they always remain undone? I have not completed the thing for which Thou hast sent me unto being, for my very creations have turned against me and the tools Thou gavest me have destroyed me. The children that I formed in love, in their ignorance have murdered me. Here, Father, is the Word Thou gavest me now red with my own blood. O Master, I return it to Thee for I have kept it sacred in my heart. Here are the tools, the tracing board, and the vessels I have wrought. Around me stand the ruins of my temple which I must leave. Unto Thee, O God, the divine Knower of all things, I return them all, realizing that in Thy good time lies the fulfillment of all things. Thou, O God, knowest our down-sitting and our uprising and Thou understandest our thoughts afar off. In Thy name, Father, I have labored and in Thy cause I die, a faithful builder."

The Master fell back, his upturned face sweet in the last repose of death, and the light rays no longer pouring from him. The gray clouds gathered closer as though to form a winding sheet around the body of their murdered Master.

Suddenly the heavens opened again, and a shaft of light bathed the form of Hiram in a glory celestial. Again the Voice spoke from the heavens where the Great King sat upon the clouds of creation: "He is not dead; he is asleep. Who will awaken him? His labors are not done, and in death he guards the sacred relics more closely than ever, for the Word and the tracing board are his — I have given them to him. But he must remain asleep until these three who have slain him shall bring him back to life, for every wrong must be righted, and the slayers of my house, the destroyers of my temple, must labor in the place of their Builder until they raise their Master from the dead."

The three murderers fell on their knees and raised their hands to heaven as though to ward off the light which had disclosed their crime: "O God, great is our sin, for we have slain our Grand Master, Hiram Abiff! Just is Thy punishment and as we have slain him we now dedicate our lives to his resurrection. The first was our human weakness, the second our sacred duty."

"Be it so," answered the Voice from Heaven. The great Light vanished and the clouds of darkness and mist concealed the body of the murdered Master. It was swallowed up in the swirling darkness which left no mark, no gravestone to mark the place where the Builder had lain.

"O God!" cried the three murderers, "where shall we find our Master now?"

A hand reached down again from the Great Unseen and a tiny lamp was handed them, whose oil flame burned silently and clearly in the darkness. "By this light shall ye seek him whom ye have slain."

The three forms surrounded the light and bowed in prayer and thanksgiving for this solitary gleam which was to light the darkness of their way. From somewhere above in the regions of not-being the great Voice spoke, a thundering Voice that filled Chaos with its sound: "He cometh forth as a flower and is cut down; he teeth also as a shadow and continueth not; as the waters fail from the sea and the flood decayeth and drieth up, so man lieth down and riseth not again. Yet have I compassion upon the children of my creation; I administer unto them in time of trouble and save them with an everlasting salvation. Seek ye where the broken twig lies and the dead stick molds away, where the clouds float together and the stones rest by the hillside, for all these mark the grave of Hiram who has carried my Will with him to the tomb. This eternal quest is yours until ye have found your Builder, until the cup giveth up its secret, until the grave giveth up its ghosts. No more shall I speak until ye have found and raised my beloved Son, and have listened to the words of my Messenger and with Him as your guide have finished the temple which I shall then inhabit. Amen."

The gray dawn still lay asleep in the arms of darkness. Out through the great mystery of not-being all was silence, unknowable. Through the misty dawn, like strange phantoms of a dream, three figures wandered over the great Unknown carrying in their hands a tiny light, the lamp given to them by their Builder's Father. Over stick and stone and cloud and star they wandered, eternally in search of a silent grave, stopping again and again to explore the depths of some mystic recess, praying for liberation from their endless search; yet bound by their vows to raise the Builder they had slain, whose grave was marked by the broken twig, and whose body was laid away in the white winding sheet of death somewhere over the brow of the eternal hill.

The Temple Builders

You are the temple builders of the future. With your hands must be raised the domes and spires of a coming civilization. Upon the foundation you have laid, tomorrow shall build a far more noble edifice. Builders of the temple of character wherein should dwell an enlightened spirit; truers of the rock of relationship; molders of those vessels created to contain the oil of life: up, and to the task appointed! Never before in the history of men have you had the opportunity that now confronts you. The world waits — waits for the illuminated one who shall come from between the pillars of the portico. Humility, hoodwinked and bound, seeks entrance to the temple of wisdom. Fling wide the gate, and let the worthy enter. Fling wide the gate, and let the light that is the life of men shine forth. Hasten to complete the dwelling of the Lord, that the Spirit of God may come and dwell among His people, sanctified and ordained according to His law.

Chapter I - The Eternal Quest

The average Mason, as well as the modern student of Masonic ideals, little realizes the cosmic obligation he takes upon himself when he begins his search for the sacred truths of Nature as they are concealed in the ancient and modern rituals. He must not lightly regard his vows, and if he would not bring upon himself years and ages of suffering he must cease to consider Freemasonry solely as a social order only a few centuries old. He must realize that the ancient mystic teachings as perpetuated in the modern rites are sacred, and that powers unseen and unrecognized mold the destiny of those who consciously and of their own free will take upon themselves the obligations of the Fraternity.

Freemasonry is not a material thing: it is a science of the soul; it is not a creed or doctrine but a universal expression of the Divine Wisdom. The coming together of medieval guilds or even the building of Solomon's temple as it is understood today has little, if anything, to do with the true origin of Freemasonry, for Masonry does not deal with personalities. In its highest sense, it is neither historical nor archaeological, but is a divine symbolic language perpetuating under certain concrete symbols the sacred mysteries of the ancients. Only those who see in it a cosmic study, a life work, a divine inspiration to better thinking, better feeling, and better living, with the spiritual attainment of enlightenment as the end, and with the daily life of the true Mason as the means, have gained even the slightest insight into the true mysteries of the ancient rites.

The age of the Masonic school is not to be calculated by hundreds or even thousands of years, for it never had any origin in the worlds of form. The world as we see it is merely an experimental laboratory in which man is laboring to build and express greater and more perfect vehicles. Into this laboratory pour myriads of rays descending from the cosmic hierarchies. These mighty globes and orbs which focus their energies upon mankind and mold its destiny do so in an orderly manner, each in its own way and place, and it is the working of these mystic hierarchies in the universe which forms the pattern around which the Masonic school has been built, for the true lodge of the Mason is the universe. Freed of limitations of creed and sect, he stands a master of all faiths, and those who take up the study of Freemasonry without realizing the depth, the beauty, and the spiritual power of its philosophy can never gain anything of permanence from their studies. The age of the Mystery Schools can be traced by the student back to the dawn of time, ages, and eons ago, when the temple of the Solar Man was in the making. That was the first Temple of the King, and therein were given and laid down the true mysteries of the ancient lodge, and it was the gods of creation and the spirits of the dawn who first tiled the Master's lodge.

The initiated brother realizes that his so called symbols and rituals are merely blinds fabricated by the wise to perpetuate ideas incomprehensible to the average individual. He also realizes that few Masons of today know or appreciate the mystic meaning concealed within these rituals. With religious faith we perpetuate the form, worshiping it instead of the life, but those who have not recognized the truth in the crystallized ritual, those who have not liberated the spiritual germ from the shell of empty words, are not Masons, regardless of their physical degrees and outward honors.

In the work we are taking up it is not the intention to dwell upon the modern concepts of the Craft but to consider Freemasonry as it really is to those who know, a great cosmic organism whose true brothers and children are tied together not by spoken oaths but by lives so lived that they are capable of seeing through the blank wall and opening the window which is now concealed by the rubbish of materiality. When this is done and the mysteries of the universe unfold before the aspiring candidate, then in truth he discovers what Freemasonry really is. Its material aspects interest him no longer for he has unmasked the Mystery School which he is capable of recognizing only when he himself has spiritually become a member of it.

Those who have examined and studied its ancient lore have no doubt that Freemasonry, like the universe itself, which is the greatest of all schools, deals with the unfolding of a threefold principle; for all the universe is governed by the same three kings who are called the builders of the Masonic temple. They are not personalities but principles, great intelligent energies, and powers which in God, man, and the universe have charge of the molding of cosmic substance into the habitation of the living king, the temple built through the ages first of unconscious and then conscious effort on the part of every individual who is expressing in his daily life the creative principles of these three kings.

The true brother of the ancient Craft realized that the completion of the temple he was building to the King of the Universe was a duty or rather a privilege which he owed to his God, to his brother, and to himself. He knew that certain steps must be taken and that his temple must be built according to the plan. Today it seems that the plan is lost, however, for in the majority of cases Freemasonry is no longer an operative art but is merely a speculative idea until each brother, reading the mystery of his symbols and pondering over the beautiful allegories unfolded in his ritual, realizes that he himself contains the keys and the plans so long lost to his Craft and that if he would ever learn Freemasonry he must unlock its doors with the key wrought from the base metals of his own being.

True Freemasonry is esoteric; it is not a thing of this world. All that we have here is a link, a doorway, through which the student may pass into the unknown. Freemasonry has nothing to do with things of form save that it realizes form is molded by and manifests the life it contains. Consequently the student is seeking so to mold his life that the form will glorify the God whose temple he is slowly building as he awakens one by one the workmen within himself and directs them to carry out the plan that has been given him out of heaven.

So far as it is possible to discover, ancient Freemasonry and the beautiful cosmic allegories that it teaches, perpetuated through hundreds of lodges and ancient mysteries, forms the oldest of the Mystery Schools; and its preservation through the ages has not depended upon itself as an exoteric body of partly evolved individuals but upon a concealed brotherhood, the exoteric side of Freemasonry. All the great Mystery Schools have hierarchies upon the spiritual planes of Nature which are expressing themselves in this world through creeds and organizations. The true student seeks to lift himself from the exoteric body upward spiritually until he joins the esoteric group which, without a lodge on the physical plane of Nature, is far greater than all the lodges of which it is the central fire. The spiritual instructors of humanity are forced to labor in the concrete world with things comprehensible to the concrete mind, and there man begins to comprehend the meaning of the allegories and symbols which surround his exoteric work as soon as he prepares himself to receive them. The true Mason realizes that the work of the Mystery Schools in the world is of an inclusive rather than an exclusive nature, and that the only lodge which is broad enough to express his ideals is one whose dome is the heavens, whose pillars are the corners of creation, whose checker-board floor is composed of the crossing currents of human emotion and whose altar is the human heart. Creeds cannot bind the true seeker for truth. Realizing the unity of all truth, the Mason also realizes that the hierarchies laboring with him have given him in his varying degrees the mystic spiritual rituals of all the Mystery Schools in the world, and if he would fill his place in the plan he must not enter this sacred study for what he can get out of it but that he may learn how to serve.

In Freemasonry is concealed the mystery of creation, the answer to the problem of existence, and the path the student must tread in order to join those who are really the living powers behind the thrones of modern national and international affairs. The true student realizes most of all that the taking of degrees does not make a man a Mason. A Mason is not appointed; he is evolved and he must realize that the position he holds in the exoteric lodge means nothing compared to his position in the spiritual lodge of life. He must forever discard the idea that he can be told or instructed in the sacred Mysteries or that his being a member of an organization improves him in any way. He must realize that his duty is to build and evolve the sacred teachings in his own being: that nothing but his own purified being can unlock the door to the sealed libraries of human consciousness, and that his Masonic rites must eternally be speculative until he makes them operative by living the life of the mystic Mason. His karmic responsibilities increase with his opportunities. Those who are surrounded with knowledge and opportunity for self-improvement and make nothing of these opportunities are the lazy workmen who will be spiritually, if not physically, cast out of the temple of the king.

The Masonic order is not a mere social organization, but is composed of all those who have banded themselves together to learn and apply the principles of mysticism and the occult rites. They are (or should be) philosophers, sages and sober-minded individuals who have dedicated themselves upon the Masonic altar and vowed by all they hold dear that the world shall be better, wiser, and happier because they have lived. Those who enter these mystic rites and pass between the pillars seeking either prestige or commercial advantage are blasphemers, and while in this world we may count them as successful, they are the cosmic failures who have barred themselves out from the true rite whose keynote is unselfishness and whose workers have renounced the things of earth.

In ancient times many years of preparation were required before the neophyte was permitted to enter the temple of the Mysteries. In this way the shallow, the curious, the faint of heart, and those unable to withstand the temptations of life were automatically eliminated by their inability to meet the requirements for admission. The successful candidate who did pass between the pillars entered the temple, keenly realizing his sublime opportunity, his divine obligation, and the mystic privilege which he had earned for himself through years of special preparation. Only those are truly Masons who enter their temple in reverence, who seek not the ephemeral things of life but the treasures which are eternal, whose sole desire is to know the true mystery of the Craft that they may join as honest workmen those who have gone before as builders of the Universal Temple. The Masonic ritual is not a ceremony, but a life to be lived. Those alone are truly Masons who, dedicating their lives and their fortunes upon the altar of the living flame, undertake the construction of the one universal building of which they are the workmen and their God the living Architect. When we have Masons like this the Craft will again be operative, the flaming triangle will shine forth with greater luster, the dead builder will rise from his tomb, and the Lost Word so long concealed from the profane will blaze forth again with the power that makes all things new.

In the pages that follow have been set down a number of thoughts for the study and consideration of temple builders, craftsmen and artisans alike. They are the keys which, if only read, will leave the student still in ignorance but, if lived, will change the speculative Masonry of today into the operative Masonry of tomorrow, when each builder, realizing his own place, will see things which he never saw before, not because they were not there but because he was blind. *And there are none so blind as those who will not see.*

THOUGHTLESSNESS

The noblest tool of the Mason is his mind, but its value is measured by the use made of it. Thoughtful in all things, the aspiring candidate to divine wisdom attains reality in sincere desire, in meditation, and in silence. Let the keynote of the Craft, and of the Ritual, be written in blazing letters: THINK OF ME. What is the meaning of this mystic maze of symbols, rites, and rituals? THINK! What does life mean, with the criss-crossings of human relationship, the endless pageantry of qualities masquerading in a carnival of fools? THINK! What is the plan behind it all, and who the planner? Where dwells the Great Architect, and what is the tracing board upon which he designs? THINK! What is the human soul, and why the endless yearning to ends unknown, along pathways where each must wander unaccompanied? Why mind, why soul, why spirit, and in truth, why anything? THINK! Is there an answer? If so, where will the truth be found? Think, Brothers of the Craft, think deeply; for if truth exists, you have it, and if truth be within the reach of living creature, what other goal is worth the struggle?

CHAPTER II - THE CANDIDATE

There comes a time in the growth of every living individual thing when it realizes with dawning consciousness that it is a prisoner. While apparently free to move and have its being, the struggling life recognizes through ever greater vehicles its own limitations. It is at this point that man cries out with greater insistence to be liberated from the binding ties which, though invisible to mortal eyes, still chain him with bonds far more terrible than those of any physical prison.

Many have read the story of the prisoner of Chillon who paced back and forth in the narrow confines of his prison cell, while the blue waters rolled ceaselessly above his head and the only sound that broke the stillness of his eternal night was the constant swishing and lapping of the waves. We pity the prisoner in his physical tomb, and we are sad at heart, for we know how life loves liberty. But there is one prisoner whose plight is far worse than those of earth. He has not even the narrow confines of a prison cell around Him; He cannot pace ceaselessly to and fro and wear ruts in the cobblestones of His dungeon floor. That eternal Prisoner is Life incarnate within the dark stone walls of matter, with not a single ray to brighten the blackness of His fate. He fights eternally, praying in the dark confines of gloomy walls for light and opportunity. This is the eternal Prisoner who, through the ceaseless ages of cosmic unfoldment, through forms unnumbered and species now unknown, strives eternally to liberate Himself and gain self-conscious expression, the birthright of every created thing. He awaits the day when, standing upon the rocks that now form His shapeless tomb, He may raise His arms to heaven, bathed in the sunlight of spiritual freedom, free to join the sparkling atoms and dancing light-beings released from the bonds of prison wall and tomb.

Around Life — that wondrous germ in the heart of every living thing, that sacred Prisoner in His gloomy cell, that Master Builder laid away in the grave of matter - has been built the wondrous legend of the Holy Sepulchre. Under allegories unnumbered, the mystic philosophers of the ages, have perpetuated this wonderful story, and among the Craft Masons it forms the mystic ritual of Hiram, the Master Builder, murdered in his temple by the very builders who should have served him as he labored to perfect the dwelling place of his God.

Matter is the tomb. It is the dead wall of substance not yet awakened into the pulsating energies of Spirit. It exists in many degrees and forms, not only in the chemical elements which form the solids of our universe but in finer and more subtle substances. These, though expressing through emotion and thought, are still beings of the world of form. These substances form the great cross of matter which opposes the growth of all things and by opposition makes all growth possible. It is the great cross of hydrogen, nitrogen, oxygen, and carbon upon which even the life germ in protoplasm is crucified and suspended in agony. These substances are incapable of giving it adequate expression. The Spirit within cries out for freedom: freedom to be, to express, to manifest its true place in the Great Plan of cosmic unfoldment.

It is this great yearning within the heart of man which sends him slowly onward toward the gate of the Temple; it is this inner urge for greater understanding and greater light which brought into being through the law of necessity the great cosmic Masonic Lodge dedicated to those seeking union with the Powers of Light that their prison walls might be removed. This shell cannot be discarded: it must be raised into union with the Life; each dead, crystallized atom in the human body must be set vibrating and spinning to a higher rate of consciousness. Through purification, through knowledge, and through service to his fellow man the candidate sequentially unfolds these mystic properties, building better and more perfect bodies through which his higher life secures even greater manifestation. The expression of man through constructive thought, emotion, and action liberates the higher nature from bodies which in their crystallized states are incapable of giving him his natural opportunities.

In Freemasonry this crystallized substance of matter is called the grave and represents the Holy Sepulchre. This is the grave within which the lost Builder lies and with Him are the plans of the Temple and the Master's Word, and it is this builder, our Grand Master, whom we must seek and raise from the dead. This noble Son of Light cries out to us in every expression of matter. Every stick and stone marks His resting place, and the sprig of acacia promises that through the long winter of spiritual darkness when the sun does not shine for man, this Light still awaits the day of liberation when each one of us shall raise Him by the grip of the Grand Master, the true grip of a Master Mason. We cannot hear this Voice that calls eternally, but we feel its inner urge. A great unknown something pulls at our heartstrings. As the ages roll by, the deep desire to be greater, to live better, and to think God's thoughts, builds within ourselves the qualifications of a candidate who, when asked why he takes the path , would truly answer if he knew mentally the things he feels: "I hear a voice that cries out to me from flora and fauna, from the stones, from the clouds, from the very heaven itself. Each fiery atom spinning and twisting in Cosmos cries out to me with the voice of my Master. I can hear Hiram Abiff, my Grand Master, crying out in his agony, the agony of life hidden within the darkness of its prison walls, seeking for the expression which I have denied it, laboring, to bring closer the day of its liberation, and I have learned to know that I am responsible for those walls. My daily actions are the things which as ruffians and traitors are murdering my God."

There are many legends of the Holy Sepulchre which for so many centuries had been in the hands of the infidel and which the Christian worlds sought to retake in the days of the Crusades. Few Masons realize that this Holy Sepulchre, or tomb, is in reality negation and crystallization — matter that has sealed within itself the Spirit of Life which must remain in darkness until the growth of each individual being gives it walls of glowing gold and changes its stones into windows. As we develop better and better vehicles of expression, these walls slowly expand until at last Spirit rises triumphant from its tomb and, blessing the very walls that confined it, raises them to union with itself.

We may first consider the murderers of Hiram. These three ruffians, who, when the Builder seeks to leave his temple, strike him with the tools of his own Craft until finally they slay him and bring the temple down in destruction upon their own heads, symbolize the three expressions of our own lower natures which are in truth the murderers of the good within ourselves. These three may be called thought, desire, and action. When purified and transmuted they are three glorious avenues through which may manifest the great life power of the three kings, the glowing builders of the Cosmic Lodge manifesting in this world as spiritual thought, constructive emotion, and useful daily labor in the various places and positions where we find ourselves while carrying on the Master's work. These three form the Flaming Triangle which glorifies every living Mason, but when crystallized and perverted they form a triangular prison through which the light cannot shine and the Life is forced to languish in the dim darkness of despair, until man himself through his higher understanding liberates the energies and powers which are indeed the builders and glorifiers of his Father's House.

Now let us consider how these three fiery kings of the dawn became, through perversion of their manifestation by man, the ruffians who murdered Hiram — the energizing powers of cosmos which course through the blood of every living being, seeking to beautify and perfect the temple they would build according to the plan laid down on the tracing board by the Master Architect of the universe. First in the mind is one of the three kings, or rather we shall say a channel through which he manifests; for King Solomon is the power of mind which, perverted, becomes a destroyer who tears down with the very powers which nourish and build. The right application of thought, when seeking the answer to the cosmic problem of destiny, liberates man's spirit which soars above the concrete through that wonderful power of mind, with its dreams and its ideals.

When man's thoughts rise upon the wings of aspiration, when he pushes back the darkness with the strength of reason and logic, then indeed the builder is liberated from his dungeon and the light pours in, bathing him with life and power. This light enables us to seek more clearly the mystery of creation and to find with greater certainty our place in the Great Plan, for as man unfolds his bodies he gains talents with which he can explore the mysteries of Nature and search for the hidden workings of the Divine. Through these powers the Builder is liberated and his consciousness goes forth conquering and to conquer. These higher ideals, these spiritual concepts, these altruistic, philanthropic, educative applications of thought power glorify the Builder; for they give the power of expression and those who can express themselves are free. When man can mold his thoughts, his emotions, and his actions into faithful expressions of his highest ideals then liberty is his, for ignorance is the darkness of Chaos and knowledge is the light of Cosmos.

In spite of the fact that many of us live apparently to gratify the desires of the body and as servants of the lower nature, still there is within each of us a power which may remain latent for a great length of time. This power lives eternities perhaps, and yet at some time during our growth there comes a great yearning for freedom, when, having discovered that the pleasures of sense gratification are eternally elusive and unsatisfying, we make an examination of ourselves and begin to realize that there are greater reasons for our being. It is sometimes reason, sometimes suffering, sometimes a great desire to be helpful, that brings out the first latent powers which show that one long wandering in the darkness is about to take the path that leads to Light. Having lived life in all its experiences, he has learned to realize that all the manifestations of being, all the various experiences through which he passes, are steps leading in one direction; that, consciously or unconsciously, all souls are being led to the portico of the temple where for the first time they see and realize the glory of Divinity. It is then that they understand the age-old allegory of the martyred Builder and feel his power within themselves crying out from the prison of materiality. Nothing else seems worthwhile; and, regardless of cost, suffering, or the taunts of the world, the candidate slowly ascends the steps that lead to the temple eternal. The reason that governs Cosmos he does not know, the laws which mold his being he does not realize, but he does know that somewhere behind the veil of human ignorance there is an eternal light toward which step by step he must labor. With his eyes fixed on the heavens above and his hands clasped in prayer he passes slowly as a candidate up the steps. In fear and trembling, yet with a divine realization of good, he raps on the door and awaits in silence the answer from within.

CHAPTER III - THE ENTERED APPRENTICE

There are three grand steps in the unfoldment of the human soul before it completes the dwelling place of the spirit. These have been caged respectively youth, manhood, and old age; or, as the Mason would say, the Entered Apprentice, the Fellow Craft, and the Master Builder. All life passes through these three grand stages of human consciousness. They can be listed as the man on the outside looking in, the man going in, and the man inside. The path of human life is governed as all things are by the laws of analogy, and as at birth we start our pilgrimage through youth, manhood, and old age, so the spiritual consciousness of man in his cosmic path of unfoldment passes from unconsciousness to perfect consciousness in the Grand Lodge of the universe. Before the initiation of the Entered Apprentice degree can be properly understood and appreciated, certain requirements must be considered, not merely those of the physical world but also those of the spiritual world.

The Mason must realize that his true initiation is a spiritual and not a physical ritual, and that his initiation into the living temple of the spiritual hierarchy regulating Freemasonry may not occur until years after he has taken the physical degree, or spiritually he may be a Grand Master before he comes into the world. There are probably few instances in the history of Freemasonry where the spiritual ordination of the aspiring seeker took place at the same time as the physical initiation, because the true initiation depends upon the cultivation of certain soul qualities — an individual and personal matter which is left entirely to the volition of the mystic Mason and which he must carry out in silence and alone.

The court of the tabernacle of the ancient Jews was divided into three parts: the outer court, the holy place, and the most Holy of Holies. These three divisions represent the three grand divisions of human consciousness. The degree of Entered Apprentice is acquired when the student signifies his intention to take the rough ashlar which he cuts from the quarry and prepares for the truing of the Fellow Craft.

In other words, the first degree is really one of preparation; it is a material step dealing with material things, for all spiritual life must be raised upon a material foundation.

Seven is the number of the Entered Apprentice as it relates to the seven liberal arts and sciences, and these are the powers with which the Entered Apprentice must labor before he is worthy to go onward into the more elevated and advanced degrees. They are much mistaken who believe that they can reach the spiritual planes of Nature without first passing through and molding matter into the expression of spiritual power; for the first stage in the growth of a Master Mason is mastery of the concrete condition s of life and the developments of sense centers which will later become channels for the expression of spiritual truths.

All growth is a gradual procedure carried on in an orderly, masterly way, as exemplified by the opening and closing of a lodge. The universe is divided into planes and these planes are divided from each other by the rates of vibration which pass through them. As the spiritual consciousness progresses through the chain, the lower lose connection with it when it has raised itself above their level, until finally only the Grand Masters are capable of remaining in session, and unknown even to the Master Mason it finally passes back again to the spiritual hierarchy from which it came.

Action is the keynote of the Entered Apprentice lodge. All growth is the result of exercise and the intensifying of vibratory rates. It is through exercise that the muscles of the human body are strengthened; it is through the seven liberal arts and sciences that the human mind receives certain impulses which, in turn, stimulate internal centers of consciousness. These centers of consciousness, through still greater development, will later give fuller expression to these inner powers; but the Entered Apprentice has for his first duty the awakening of these powers, and, like the youth of whom he is a symbol, his ideals and labors must be tied closely to concrete things. For him both points of the compasses are under the square; for him the reasons which manifest through the heart and mind — the two polarities of expression are darkened and concealed beneath the square which measures the block of bodies. He knows not the reason why; his work is to follow the directions of those whose knowledge is greater than his own; but as the result of the application of energies, through action and reaction he slowly builds and evolves the powers of discrimination and the strength of character which mark the Fellow Craft degree.

It is obvious that the rough ashlar symbolizes the body. It also represents cosmic root substance which is taken out of the quarry of the universe by the first expressions of intelligence and molded by them into ever finer and more perfect lines until finally it becomes the perfect stone for the Builder's temple.

How can emotion manifest save through form? How can mind manifest until the intricately evolved brain cells of matter have raised their organic quality to form the ground-work upon which other things may be based? All students of human nature realize that every expression of man depends upon organic quality; that in every living thing this differs; and that the fineness of this matter is the certain indication of growth — mental, physical, or spiritual.

True to the doctrines of his Craft, the Entered Apprentice must beautify his temple. He must build within himself by his actions, by the power of his hand and the tools of his Craft, certain qualities which make possible his initiation into the higher degrees of the spiritual lodge.

We know that the cube block is symbolic of the tomb. It is also well known that the Entered Apprentice is incapable of rolling away the stone or of transmuting it into a greater or higher thing; but it is his privilege to purify and glorify that stone and begin the great work of preparing it for the temple of his King.

Few realize that since the universe is made up of individuals in various stages of development, responsibility is consequently individual, and everything which man wishes to gain he must himself build and maintain. If he is to use his finer bodies for the purpose for which they were intended, he must treat them well, that they may be good and faithful servants in the great work he is preparing for.

The quarries represent the limitless powers of natural resources. They are symbolic of the practically endless field of human opportunity; they symbolize the cosmic substances from which man must gather the stones for his temple. At this stage in his growth, the Entered Apprentice is privileged to gather the stones which he wishes to true during his progress through the lodge, for at this point he symbolizes the youth who is choosing his life work. He represents the human ego who in the dawn of time gathered many blocks and cubes and broken stones from the Great Quarry. These rough and broken stones that as yet will not fit into anything are the partially evolved powers and senses with which he labors. In the first state he must gather these materials, and those who have not gathered them can never true them. During the involuntary period of human consciousness, the Entered Apprentice in the Great Lodge was man, who labored with these rough blocks, seeking the tools and the power with which to true them. As he evolves down through the ages, he gains the tools and cosmically passes on to the degree of Fellow Craft where he trues his ashlar in harmony with the plans upon the Master's tracing board. This rough, uncut ashlar has three dimensions, representative of the three ruffians who at this stage are destroyers of the fourth dimensional life concealed within the ugly, ill-shaped stone.

The lost key of the Entered Apprentice is service. Why, he may not ask; when, he does not know. His work is to do, to act, to express himself in some way — constructively if possible, but destructively rather than not at all. Without action, he loses his great work; without tools, which symbolize the body, he cannot act in an organized manner. Consequently, it is necessary to master the arts and sciences which place in his hands intelligent tools for the expression of energy. Beauty is the keynote to his ideal. With his concrete ideals he must beautify all with which he comes in contact, so that the works of his hand may be acceptable in the eyes of the Great Architect of the Universe.

His daily life, in home, business, and society, together with the realization of the fundamental unity of each with all, form the base upon which the aspiring candidate may raise a greater superstructure. In truth he must live the life, the result of which is the purification of his body, so that the more attenuated forces of the higher degrees may express themselves through the finer sensitivity of the receiving pole within himself. When he reaches this stage in his growth, he is spiritually worthy to consider advancement into a higher degree. This advancement is not the result of election or ballot, but is an automatic process in which, having sensitized his consciousness by his life, he thereby attunes himself to the next succeeding plane of expression. All initiation is the result of adjustments of the evolving life to the physical, emotional, and mental planes of consciousness through which it passes.

We may now consider the spiritual requirements of one who feels that he would mystically correlate himself with that great spiritual fraternity which, concealed behind the exoteric rite, forms the living power of the Entered Apprentice lodge:

1. It is essential that the Entered Apprentice should have studied sufficiently the subject of anatomy to have at least a general idea of the physical body, for the entire degree is based upon the mystery of form. The human body is the highest manifestation of form which he is capable of analyzing. Consequently, he must devote himself to the study of his own being and its mysteries and complexities.

2. The Entered Apprentice must realize that his body is the living temple of the living God and treat it accordingly; for when he abuses or mistreats it he breaks the sacred obligations which he must assume before he can ever hope to understand the true mysteries of the Craft. The breaking of his pact with the higher Life evolving within himself unfailingly invokes the retributive agencies of Nature.

3. He must study the problem of the maintenance of bodies through food, clothing, breathing, and other necessities, as all of these are important steps in the Entered Apprentice lodge. Those who eat immoderately, dress improperly, and use only about one-third of their lung capacity can never have the physical efficiency necessary for the fullest expression of the higher Life.

4. He must grow physically and in the expression of concrete things. Human relationships must be idealized at this time, and he must seek to unfold all unselfish qualities which are necessary for the harmonious working of the Mason and his fellow men on the physical plane of Nature.

5. He must seek to round off all inequalities. He can best do this by balancing his mental and physical organisms through the application and study of the seven liberal arts and sciences.

Until he is relatively master of these principles on the highest plane within his own being, he cannot hope spiritually to attract to himself, through the qualities of his own character, the life-giving ray of the Fellow Craft. When he reaches this point, however, he is spiritually ready to hope for membership in a more advanced degree.

The Mason must realize that his innermost motives are the index of his real self, and those who allow social position, financial or business considerations or selfish and materialistic ideals, to lead them into the Masonic Brotherhood have thereby automatically separated themselves from the Craft. They can never do any harm to Freemasonry by joining because they cannot get in. Ensconced within the lodge, they may feel that they have deceived the Grand Master of the Universe, but when the spiritual lodge meets to carry on the true work of the Craft, they are disqualified and absent. Watch fobs, lapel badges, and other insignia do not make Masons; neither does the ritual ordain them. Masons are evolved through the self-conscious effort to live up to the highest ideals within themselves; their lives are the sole insignia of their rank, greater by far than any visible, tangible credential.

Bearing this in mind, it is possible for the unselfish, aspiring soul to become spiritually and liberally vouched for by the centers of consciousness as an Entered Apprentice. It means he has taken the first grand step on the path of personal liberation. He is now symbolized as the child with the smiling face, for with the simplicity of a child he places himself under the protection of his great spiritual Father, willing and glad to obey each of His commands. Having reached this point and having done the best it was possible for him to do, he is in position to hope that the powers that be, moving in their mysterious manner, may find him worthy to undertake the second great step in spiritual liberation.

Chapter IV - The Fellow Craft

Life manifests not only through action on the physical plane, but through human emotion and sentiment. This is the type of energy taken up by the student when he starts his labors in the Fellow Craft. From youth with its smiling face, he passes on to the greater responsibilities of manhood.

On the second step of the temple stands a soldier dressed in shining armor, but his sword is sheathed and a book is in his hand. He is symbolic of strength, the energy of Mars, and the wonderful step in spiritual unfoldment which we know as Fellow Craft. Through each one of us course the fiery rays of human emotion, a great seething cauldron of power behind each expression of human energy. Like spirited horses chafing at the bit, like hounds eager for the chase, the emotional powers cannot be held in check, but break the walls of restraint and pour forth as fiery expressions of dynamic energy. This great principle of emotion we know as the second murderer of Hiram. Through the perversion of human emotions there comes into the world untold sorrow, which through reaction, manifests in the mental and physical bodies.

It is strange how divine powers may become perverted until each expression and urge becomes a ruffian and a murderer. The divine compassion of the gods manifests in this world of form very differently than in the realms of light. Divine compassion is energized by the same influxes as mortal passions and the lusts of earth. The spiritual light rays of Cosmos — the Fire Princes of the Dawn — which seethe and surge through the unregenerate man, are the impulses which he perverts to murder and hate. The ceaseless power of Chaos, the seething pinwheel of perpetual motion, whose majestic cadences are the music of the spheres, are energized by the same great power that man uses to destroy the highest and best. The same mystic power that keeps the planets in their orbits around the solar body, the same energy that keeps each electron spinning and whirling, the same energy that is building the temple of God, is now a merciless slave-driver which , unmastered and uncurbed, strikes the Compassionate One and sends him reeling backward into the darkness of his prison. Man does not listen to that little voice which speaks to him in ever loving, ever sorrowful tones. This voice speaks of the peace accompanying the constructive application of energy which he must chain if he would master the powers of creation. How long will it take King Hiram of Tyre, the warrior on the second step, symbolic of the Fellow Craft of the Cosmic Lodge, to teach mankind the lessons of self-mastery? The teacher can do it only as he daily depicts the miseries which are the result of uncurbed appetites. The strength of man was not given to be used destructively but that he might build a temple worthy to be the dwelling place of the Great Architect of the universe. God is glorifying himself through the individualized portions of himself, and is slowly teaching these individualized portions to understand and glorify the whole.

The day has come when Fellow Craftsmen must know and apply their knowledge. The lost key to their grade is the mastery of emotion, which places the energy of the universe at their disposal. Man can only expect to be entrusted with great power by proving his ability to use it constructively and selflessly. When the Mason learns that the key to the warrior on the block is the proper application of the dynamo of living power, he has learned the mystery of his Craft. The seething energies of Lucifer are in his hands and before he may step onward and upward, he must prove his ability to properly apply energy. He must follow in the footsteps of his forefather, Tubal-Cain, who with the mighty strength of the war god hammered his sword into a plowshare. Incessant vigilance over thought, action, and desire is indispensable to those who wish to make progress in the unfolding of their own being, and the Fellow Craft's degree is the degree of transmutation.

The hand that slays must lift the fallen, while the lips given to cursing must be taught to pray. The heart that hates must learn the mystery of compassion, as the result of a deeper and more perfect understanding of man's relation to his brother. The firm, kind hand of spirit must curb the flaming powers of emotion with an iron grip. In the realization and application of these principles lies the key of the Fellow Craft.

In this degree, the two points of the compass (one higher than the other), symbolize the heart and mind, and with the expression of the higher emotions the heart point of the compass is liberated from the square, which is an instrument used to measure the block of matter and therefore symbolizes form.

A large percentage of the people of the world at the present time are passing through, spiritually, the degree of the Fellow Craft, with its five senses. The sense perceptions come under the control of the emotional energies; therefore the development of the senses is necessary to the constructive expression of the Fellow Craft power. Man must realize that all the powers which his many years of need have earned for him have come in order that through them he may liberate more fully the prisoner within his own being. As the Fellow Craft degree is the middle of the three, the spiritual duty of each member is to reach the point of poise or balance, which is always secured between extremes. The mastery of expression is also to be found in this degree. The keywords of the Fellow Craft may be briefly defined as compassion, poise, and transmutation.

In the Fellow Craft degree is concealed the dynamo of human life. The Fellow Craft is the worker with elemental fire, which it is his duty to transmute into spiritual light. The heart is the center of his activity, and it is while in this degree that the human side of nature with its constructive emotions should be brought out and emphasized. But all of these expressions of the human heart must become transmuted into the emotionless compassion of the gods, who despite the suffering of the moment, gaze down upon mankind and see that it is good.

When the candidate feels that he has reached a point where he is able to manifest every energizing current and fire-flame in a constructive, balanced manner and has spiritually lifted the heart sentiments of the mystic out of the cube of matter, he may then expect that the degree of Master Mason is not far off, and so may look forward eagerly to the time of his spiritual ordination into the higher degree. He should now study himself and realize that he cannot receive promotion into the spiritual lodge until his heart is attuned to a superior, spiritual influx from the causal planes of consciousness.

The following requirements are necessary before the student can spiritually say that he is a member of the ancient and accepted rite of the Fellow Craft:

1. The mastery of emotional outbreaks of all kinds, poise under trying conditions, kindness in the face of unkindness, and simplicity with its accompanying power. These points show that the seeker is worthy of being taught by a Fellow Craftsman.

2. The mastery of the animal energies, the curbing of passion and desire, and the control of the lower nature mark the faithful attempts on the part of the student to be worthy of the Fellow Craft.

3. The understanding and mastery of the creative forces, the consecration of them to the unfolding of the spiritual nature, and a proper understanding of their physical application, are necessary steps at this stage of the student's growth.

4. The transmutation of personal affection into impersonal compassion shows that the Fellow Craftsman truly understands his duties and is living in a manner worthy of his order. Personalities cannot bind the true second degree member, for having raised one point of the compasses he now realizes that all personal manifestations are governed by impersonal principles.

5. At this point the candidate consecrates the five senses to the study of human problems with the unfolding of sense centers as the motive; for he realizes that the five senses are keys, the proper application of which will give him material for spiritual transmutation if he applies to them the common divisor of analogy.

The Entered Apprentice may be termed a materialistic degree. The Fellow Craft is religious and mystical, while the Master Mason is occult or philosophical. Each of these is a degree in the unfoldment of a connected life and intelligence, revealing in ever-fuller expression the gradual liberation of the Master from the triangular cell of threefold negation which marks the early stage of individualization.

Chapter V - The Master Mason

On the upper steps of spiritual unfoldment stands the Master Mason, who spiritually represents the graduate from the school of esoteric learning. In the ancient symbols he is represented as an old man leaning upon a staff, his long white beard upon his chest, and his deep, piercing eyes sheltered by the brows of a philosopher. He is in truth old, not in years, but in wisdom and understanding, which are the only true measurement of age. Through years and lives of labor he has found the staff of life and truth upon which he leans. He no longer depends upon the words of others but upon the still voice that speaks from the heart of his own being. There is no more glorious position that a man may hold than that of a Master Builder, who has risen by labor through the degrees of human consciousness. Time is the differentiation of eternity devised by man to measure the passage of human events. On the spiritual planes of Nature it is the space or distance between the stages of spiritual growth and hence is not measurable by material means. Many a child comes into this world a Grand Master of the Masonic School, while many a revered and honored brother passes silently to rest without having gained admittance to its gate. The Master Mason is one whose life is full, pressed down and brimming over with the experience he has gained in his slow pilgrimage up the winding stairs.

The Master Mason embodies the power of the human mind, that connecting link which binds heaven and earth together in an endless chain. His spiritual light is greater because he has evolved a higher vehicle for its expression. Above even constructive action and emotion soars the power of thought which swiftly flies on wings to the source of Light. The mind is the highest form of his human expression, and he passes into the great darkness of the inner room illuminated only by the fruits of reason. The glorious privileges of a Master Mason are in keeping with his greater knowledge and wisdom. From the student he has blossomed forth as the teacher; from the kingdom of those who follow he has joined that little group who must always lead the way. For him the Heavens have opened and the Great Light has bathed him in its radiance. The Prodigal Son, so long a wanderer in the regions of darkness, has returned again to his Father's house.

The voice speaks from the Heavens, its power thrilling the Master until his own being seems filled with its divinity, saying, "This is my beloved Son, in whom I am well pleased." The ancients taught that the sun was not a source of light, life, or power, but a medium through which life and light were reflected into physical substance. The Master Mason is in truth a sun, a great reflector of light, who radiates through his organism, purified by ages of preparation, the glorious power which is the light of the Lodge. He, in truth, has become the spokesman of the Most High. He stands between the glowing fire light and the world. Through him passes Hydra, the great snake, and from its mouth there pours to man the light of God. His symbol is the rising sun, for in him the globe of day has indeed risen in all its splendor from the darkness of the night, illuminating the immortal East with the first promise of approaching day.

With a sigh the Master lays aside his tools. For him the temple is nearing completion, the last stones are being placed, and he slakes his limestone with a vague regret as he sees dome and minaret rise through the power of his handiwork. The true Master does not long for rest, and as he sees the days of his labor close, a sadness weighs upon his heart. Slowly the brothers of his Craft leave him, each going his respective way; and, climbing step by step, the Master stands alone on the pinnacle of the temple. One stone must yet be placed, but this he cannot find. Somewhere it lies concealed. In prayer he kneels, asking the powers that be to aid him in his search. The light of the sun shines upon him and bathes him in a splendor celestial. Suddenly a voice speaks from the Heavens, saying, "The temple is finished and in my faithful Master is found the missing stone."

Both points of the compasses are now lifted from under the square. The divine is liberated from its cube; heart and mind alike are liberated from the symbol of mortality, and as emotion and thought they unite for the glorification of the greatest and the highest. Then the Sun and Moon are united, and the Hermetic Degree is consummated.

The Master Mason is afforded opportunities far beyond the reach of ordinary man, but he must not fail to realize that with every opportunity comes a cosmic responsibility. It is worse by far to know and not to do than never to have known at all. He realizes that the choice of avoiding responsibility is no longer his and that for him all problems must be met and solved. The only joy in the heart of the Master is the joy of seeing the fruits of his handiwork. It can be truly said of the Master that through suffering he has learned to be glad, through weeping he has learned to smile, and through dying he has learned to live. The purification and probationship of his previous degrees have so spiritualized his being that he is in truth a glorious example of God's Plan for His children. The greatest sermon he can preach, the greatest lesson he can teach, is that of standing forth a living proof of the Eternal Plan. The Master Mason is not ordained: he is the natural product of cause and effect, and none but those who live the cause can produce the effect. The Master Mason, if he be truly a Master, is in communication with the unseen powers that move the destinies of life. As the Eldest Brother of the lodge, he is the spokesman for the spiritual hierarchies of his Craft. He no longer follows the direction of others, but on his own tracing board he lays out the plans which his brothers are to follow. He realizes this, and so lives that every line and plan which he gives out is inspired by the divine within himself. His glorious opportunity to be a factor in the growth of others comes before all else. At the seat of mercy he kneels, a faithful servant of the Highest within himself and worthy to be given control over the lives of others by having first controlled himself.

Much is said concerning the loss of the Master's Word and how the seekers go out to find it but bring back only substitutes. The true Master knows that those who go out can never find the secret trust. He alone can find it who goes within. The true Master Builder has never lost the Word but has cherished it in the spiritual locket of his own being. From those who have the eyes to see, nothing is concealed; to those who have the right to know, all things are open books. The true Word of the three Grand Masters has never been concealed from those who have the right to know it nor has it ever been revealed to those who have not prepared a worthy shrine to contain it. The Master knows, for he is a Temple Builder. Within the setting of his own bodies, the Philosopher's Stone is placed; for in truth it is the heart of the Phoenix, that strange bird which rises with renewed youth from the ashes of its burned body. When the Master's heart is as pure and white as the diamond that he wears, he will then become a living stone — the crown jewel in the diadem of his Craft.

The Word is found when the Master himself is ordained by the living hand of God, cleansed by living water, baptized by living fire, a Priest-King after the Order of Melchizedek, who is above the law.

The great work of the Master Mason can be called the art of balance. To him is given the work of balancing the triangle that it may blaze forth with the glory of the Divine Degree. The triple energies of thought, desire, and action must be united in a harmonious blending of expression. He holds in his hands the triple keys; he wears the triple crown of the ancient Magus, for he is in truth the King of heaven, earth, and hell. Salt, Sulphur, and mercury are the elements of his work and with the philosophical mercury he seeks to blend all powers to the glorifying of one end.

Behind the degree of Master Mason, there is another not known to earth. Far above him stretch other steps concealed by the blue veil which divides the seen from the unseen. The true Brother knows this, therefore he works with an end in view far above the concept of mortal mind. He seeks to be worthy to pass behind that veil and join that band who, unhonored and unsung, carry the responsibilities of human growth. His eyes are fixed forever on the Seven Stars which shine down from somewhere above the upper rung of the ladder. With hope, faith, and charity he climbs the steps, and whispering the Master's Word to the Keeper of the Gates, passes on behind the veil. It is then, and then only, that a true Mason is born. Only behind this veil does the mystic student come into his own. The things which we see around us are but forms — promises of a thing unnamed, symbols of a truth unknown. It is in the spiritual temple built without the voice of workmen or the sound of hammer that the true initiation is given, and there, robed in the simple lambskin of a purified body, the student becomes a Master Mason, chosen out of the world to be an active worker in the name of the Great Architect. It is there alone, unseen by mortal eyes, that the Greater Degrees are given and there the soul radiating the light of Spirit becomes a living star in the blue canopy of the Masonic lodge.

Transmutation

Masonry is eternal truth, personified, idealized, and yet made simple. Eternal truth alone can serve it. Virtue is its priest, patience its warden, illumination its master. The world cannot know this, however, save when Masons in their daily life prove that it is so. Its truth is divine, and is not to be desecrated or defamed by the thoughtlessness of its keepers. Its temple is a holy place, to be entered in reverence. Material thoughts and material dissensions must be left without its gate. They may not enter. Only the pure of heart, regenerated and transmuted, may pass the sanctity of its veil. The schemer has no place in its ranks, nor the materialist in its shrine; for Masons walk on hallowed ground, sanctified by the veneration of ages. Let the tongue be stilled, let the heart be stilled, let the mind be stilled. In reverence and in the silence, stillness shall speak: the voice of stillness is the voice of the Creator. Show your light and your power to men, but before God what have you to offer, save in humility? Your robes, your tinsel, and your jewels mean naught to Him, until your own body and soul, gleaming with the radiance of perfection, become the living ornaments of your Lodge.

THE PRESENCE OF THE MASTER

The Mason believes in the Great Architect, the living keystone of creation's plan, the Master of all Lodges, without whose spirit there is no work. Let him never forget that the Master is near. Day and night let him feel the presence of the Supreme or Overshadowing One. The All-Seeing Eye is upon him. Day and night this great Orb measures his depths, seeing into his innermost soul of souls, judging his life, reading his thoughts, measuring his aspirations, and rewarding his sincerity. To this All-Seeing One he is accountable; to none other must he account. This Spirit passes with him out of the Lodge and measures the Mason in the world. This Spirit is with him when he buys and sells. It is with him in his home. By the light of day and by the darkness of night it judges him. It hears each thoughtless word. It is the silent witness to every transaction of life, the silent Partner of every man. By the jury of his acts, each man is judged. Let every Mason know that his obligations include not only those within the narrow Lodge, bordered by walls of stone and brick, but those in the Great Lodge, walled only by the dome of heaven. The Valley of Jehoshaphat waits for him who is false to any creature, as surely as it waited for the breakers of the Cosmic oath.

CHAPTER VI - THE QUALIFICATIONS OF A TRUE MASON

Every true Mason has come into the realization that there is but one Lodge — that is, the Universe — and but one Brotherhood, composed of everything that moves or exists in any of the planes of Nature. He realizes that the Temple of Solomon is really the Temple of the Solar Man — Sol-Om-On — the King of the Universe manifesting through his three primordial builders. He realizes that his vow of brotherhood and fraternity is universal, and that mineral, plant, animal, and man are all included in the true Masonic Craft. His duty as an elder brother to all the kingdoms of Nature beneath him is well understood by the true Craftsman, who would rather die than fail in this, his great obligation. He has dedicated his life upon the altar of his God and is willing and glad to serve the lesser through the powers he has gained from the greater. The mystic Mason, in building the eyes that see behind the apparent ritual, recognizes the oneness of life manifesting through the diversity of form.

The true disciple of ancient Masonry has given up forever the worship of personalities. With his greater insight, he realizes that all forms and their position in material affairs are of no importance to him compared to the life which is evolving within. Those who allow appearances or worldly expressions to deter them from their self-appointed tasks are failures in Masonry, for Masonry is an abstract science of spiritual unfoldment. Material prosperity is not the measure of soul growth. The true Mason realizes that behind these diverse forms there is one connected Life Principle, the spark of God in all living things. It is this Life which he considers when measuring the worth of a brother. It is to this Life that he appeals for a recognition of spiritual Unity. He realizes that it is the discovery of this spark of Unity which makes him a conscious member of the Cosmic Lodge. Most of all, he must learn to understand that this divine spark shines out as brightly from the body of a foe as it does from the dearest friend. The true Mason has learned to be divinely impersonal in thought, action, and desire.

The true Mason is not creed-bound. He realizes with the divine illumination of his lodge that as Mason his religion must be universal: Christ, Buddha or Mohammed, the name means little, for he recognizes only the light and not the bearer. He worships at every shrine, bows before every altar, whether in temple, mosque, or cathedral, realizing with his truer understanding the oneness of all spiritual truth. All true Masons know that they only are heathen who, having great ideals, do not live up to them. They know that all religions are but one story told in different ways for peoples whose ideals differ but whose great purpose is in harmony with Masonic ideals. North, east, south and west stretch the diversities of human thought, and while the ideals of man apparently differ, when all is said and the crystallization of form with its false concepts is swept away, one basic truth remains: all existing things are Temple Builders, laboring for a single end. No true Mason can be narrow, for his Lodge is the divine expression of all broadness. There is no place for little minds in a great work.

The true Mason must develop the powers of observation. He must seek eternally in all the manifestations of Nature for the things which he has lost because he failed to work for them. He must become a student of human nature and see in those around him the unfolding and varying expressions of one connected spiritual Intelligence. The great spiritual ritual of his lodge is enacted before him in every action of his fellow man. The entire Masonic initiation is an open secret, for anyone can see it played out on the city street corners as well as in the untracked wilderness. The Mason has sworn that every day he will extract from life its message for him and build it into the temple of his God. He seeks to learn the things which will make him of greater service in the Divine Plan, a better instrument in the hands of the Great Architect, who is laboring eternally to unfold life through the medium of living things. The Mason realizes, moreover, that his vows, taken of his own free will and accord, give him the divine opportunity of being a living tool in the hands of a Master Workman.

The true Master Mason enters his lodge with one thought uppermost in his mind: "How can I, as an individual, be of greater use in the Universal Plan? What can I do to be worthy to comprehend the mysteries which are unfolded here? How can I build the eyes to see the things which are concealed from those who lack spiritual understanding?" The true Mason is supremely unselfish in every expression and application of the powers that have been entrusted to him. No true Brother seeks anything for himself, but unselfishly labors for the good of all. No person who assumes a spiritual obligation for what he can get out of it is worthy of applying for the position even of water-carrier. The true Light can come only to those who, asking nothing, gladly give all to it.

The true brother of the Craft, while constantly striving to improve himself, mentally, physically, and spiritually through the days of his life, never makes his own desires the goal for his works. He has a duty and that duty is to fit into the plans of another. He must be ready at any hour of the day or night to drop his own ideals at the call of the Builder. The work must be done and he has dedicated his life to the service of those who know the bonds of neither time nor space. He must be ready at any moment's notice and his life should be turned into preparing himself for that call which may come when he least expects it. The Master Mason knows that those most useful to the Plan are those who have gained the most from the practical experiences of life. It is not what goes on within the tiled lodge which is the basis of his greatness, but rather the way in which he meets the problems of daily life. The true Masonic student is known by his brotherly actions and common sense.

Every Mason knows that a broken vow brings with it a terrible penalty. Let him also realize that failure to live mentally, spiritually, and morally up to one's highest ideals constitutes the greatest of all broken oaths. When a Mason swears that he will devote his life to the building of his Father's house and then defiles his living temple through the perversion of mental power, emotional force, and active energy, he is breaking a vow which imposes not hours but ages of misery. If he is worthy to be a Mason, he must be great enough to restrain the lower side of his own nature which is daily murdering his Grand Master. He must realize that a misdirected life is a broken vow and that daily service, purification, and the constructive application of energy is a living invocation which builds within and draws to him the power of the Creator. His life is the only prayer acceptable in the eyes of the Most High. An impure life is a broken trust; a destructive action is a living curse; a narrow mind is a strangle-cord around the throat of God.

All true Masons know that their work is not secret, but they realize that it must remain unknown to all who do not live the true Masonic life. Yet if the so-called secrets of Freemasonry were shouted from the housetops, the Fraternity would be absolutely safe; for certain spiritual qualities are necessary before the real Masonic secrets can be understood by the brethren themselves. Hence it is that the alleged "exposures" of Freemasonry, printed by the thousands and tens of thousands since 1730 down to the present hour, cannot injure the Fraternity. They reveal merely the outward forms and ceremonies of Freemasonry. Only those who have been weighed in the balance and found to be true, upright, and square have prepared themselves by their own growth to appreciate the inner meanings of their Craft. To the rest of their brethren within or without the lodge their sacred rituals must remain, as Shakespeare might have said, "Words, words, words." Within the Mason's own being is concealed the Power, which, blazing forth from his purified being, constitutes the Builder's Word. His life is the sole password which admits him to the true Masonic Lodge. His spiritual urge is the sprig of acacia which, through the darkness of ignorance, still proves that the spiritual fire is alight. Within himself he must build those qualities which will make possible his true understanding of the Craft. He can show the world only forms which mean nothing; the life within is forever concealed until the eye of Spirit reveals it.

The Master Mason realizes charity to be one of the greatest traits which the Elder Brothers have unfolded, which means not only properly regulated charity of the purse but charity in thought and action. He realizes that all the workmen are not on the same step, but wherever each may be, he is doing the best he can according to his light. Each is laboring with the tools that he has, and he, as a Master Mason, does not spend his time in criticizing but in helping them to improve their tools. Instead of blaming poor tools, let us always blame ourselves for having them. The Master Mason does not find fault; he does not criticize nor does he complain, but with malice towards none and charity towards all he seeks to be worthy of his Father's trust. In silence he labors, with compassion he suffers, and if the builders strike him as he seeks to work with them, his last word will be a prayer for them. The greater the Mason, the more advanced in his Craft, the more fatherly he grows, the walls of his Lodge broadening out until all living things are sheltered and guarded within the blue folds of his cape. From laboring with the few he seeks to assist all, realizing with his broader understanding the weaknesses of others but the strength of right.

A Mason is not proud of his position. He is not puffed up by his honor, but with a sinking heart is eternally ashamed of his own place, realizing that it is far below the standard of his Craft. The farther he goes, the more he realizes that he is standing on slippery places and if he allows himself for one moment to lose his simplicity and humility, a fall is inevitable. A true Mason never feels himself worthy of his Craft. A student may stand on the top of Fool's Mountain self-satisfied in his position, but the true Brother is always noted for his simplicity.

A Mason cannot be ordained or elected by ballot. He is evolved through ages of self-purification and spiritual transmutation. There are thousands of Masons who are brethren in name only, for their failure to exemplify the ideals of their Craft makes them unresponsive to the teachings and purpose of Freemasonry. The Masonic life forms the first key of the Temple and without this key, none of the doors can be opened. When this fact is better realized and lived, Freemasonry will awake, and speak the Word so long withheld. The speculative Craft will then become operative, and the Ancient Wisdom so long concealed will rise from the ruins of its temple as the greatest spiritual truth yet revealed to man.

The true Master Mason recognizes the value of seeking for truth wherever he can find it. It makes no difference if it be in the enemy's camp; if it be truth, he will go there gladly to secure it. The Masonic Lodge is universal; therefore all true Masons will seek through the extremities of creation for their Light. The true brother of the Craft knows and applies one great paradox. He must search for the high things in lowly places and find the lowly things in high places. The Mason who feels holier than his fellow man has raised a barrier around himself through which no light can pass, for the one who in truth is the greatest is the servant of all. Many brethren make a great mistake in building a wall around their secrets, for they succeed only in shutting out their own light. Their divine opportunity is at hand. The time has come when the world needs the Ancient Wisdom as never before. Let the Mason stand forth and by living the doctrines which he preaches show to his brother man the glory of his work. He holds the keys to truth; let him unlock the door, and with his life and not his words preach the doctrine which he has so long professed.

The Fatherhood of God and the Brotherhood of Man were united in the completion of the Eternal Temple, the Great Work, for which all things came into being and through which all shall glorify their Creator.

Masons, Awake!

Your creed and your Craft demand the best that is in you. They demand the sanctifying of your life, the regeneration of your body, the purification of your soul, and the ordination of your spirit. Yours is the glorious opportunity; yours is the divine responsibility. Accept your task and follow in the footsteps of the Master Masons of the past, who with the flaming spirit of the Craft have illumined the world. You have a great privilege — the privilege of enlightened labor. You may know the ends to which you work, while others must struggle in darkness. Your labors are not to be confined to the tiled Lodge alone, for a Mason must radiate the qualities of his Craft. Its light must shine in his home and in his business, glorifying his association with his fellow men. In the Lodge and out of the Lodge, the Mason must represent the highest fruitage of sincere endeavor.

Epilogue
The Priest of Ra

What words are there in modern language to describe the great temple of Ammon Ra? It now stands amidst the sands of Egypt a pile of broken ruins, but in the heyday of its glory it rose a forest of plumed pillars holding up roofs of solid sandstone, carved by hands long laid to rest into friezes of lotus blossoms and papyrus and colored lifelike by pigments the secrets of which were lost with the civilization that discovered them. A checkerboard floor of black and white blocks stretched out until it was lost among the wilderness of pillars. From the massive walls the impassive faces of gods unnamed looked down upon the silent files of priests who kept alight the altar fires, whose feeble glow alone alighted the massive chambers throughout the darkness of an Egyptian night. It was a weird, impressive scene, and the flickering lights sent strange, ghostly forms scurrying among the piles of granite which rose like mighty altars from the darkness below to be lost in the shadows above.

Suddenly a figure emerged from the shadows, carrying in his hand a small oil lamp which pierced the darkness like some distant star, bringing into strange relief the figure of him who bore it. He appeared to be old, for his long beard and braided hair were quite gray, but his large black eyes shone with a fire seldom seen even in youth. He was robed from head to foot in blue and gold, and around his forehead was coiled a snake of precious metal, set with jeweled eyes that gave out flashes of light. Never had the light of Ra's chamber shone on a grander head or a form more powerful than that of the high priest of the temple. He was the mouthpiece of the gods and the sacred wisdom of ancient Egypt was impressed in fiery letters upon his soul. As he crossed the great room — in one hand the scepter of the priestcraft, in the other the tiny lamp — he was more like a spirit visitor from beyond the environs of death than a physical being, for his jeweled sandals made no sound and the sheen from his robes formed a halo of light around his stately form.

Down through the silent passageways, lined with their massive pillars, passed the phantom figure — down steps lined with kneeling sphinxes and through avenues of crouching lions the priest picked his way until at last he reached a vaulted chamber whose marble floor bore strange designs traced in some language long forgotten. Each angle of the many-sided and dimly-lighted room was filled by a seated figure carved in stone, so massive that its head and shoulders were lost in shadows no eye could pierce.

In the center of this mystic chamber stood a great chest of some black stone carved with serpents and strange winged dragons. The lid was a solid slab, weighing hundreds of pounds, without handle of any kind and the chest apparently had no means of being opened without the aid of some herculean power.

The high priest leaned over and from the lamp he carried lighted the fire upon an altar that stood near, sending the shadows of that weird chamber scurrying into the most distant corners. As the flame rose, it was reflected from the great stone faces above, which seemed to stare at the black coffer in the center of the room with their strange, sightless eyes.

Raising his serpent-wound staff and facing the chest of sombre marble, the priest called out in a voice that echoed and re-echoed from every nook and cranny of the ancient temple:

"Aradamas, come forth!"

Then a strange thing happened. The heavy slab that formed the cover of the great coffer slowly raised as though lifted by unseen hands and there emerged from its dark recesses a slim, white-clad figure with his forearms crossed on his breast-the figure of a man perhaps thirty years old, his long, black hair hanging down upon his white-robed shoulders in strange contrast to the seamless garment that he wore. His face, devoid of emotion, was as handsome and serene as the great face of Ammon Ra himself that gazed down upon the scene. Silently Aradamas stepped from the ancient tomb and advanced slowly toward the high priest. When about ten paces from the earthly representative of the gods, he paused, unfolded his arms, and extended them across his chest in salutation. In one hand he carried a cross with a ring as the upper arm and this he proffered to the priest. Aradamas stood in silence as the high priest, raising his scepter to one of the great stone figures, addressed an invocation to the Sun-God of the universe. This finished, he then addressed the youthful figure as follows:

"Aradamas, you seek to know the mystery of creation, you ask that the divine illumination of the Thrice-Greatest and the wisdom that for ages has been the one gift the gods would shower upon mankind, be entrusted to you. Little you understand of the thing you ask, but those who know have said that he who proves worthy may receive the truth. Therefore, stand you here today to prove your divine birthright to the teaching that you ask."

The priest pronounced these words slowly and solemnly and then pointed with his scepter to a great dim archway surmounted by a winged globe of gleaming gold.

"Before thee, up those steps and through those passageways, lies the path that leads to the eye of judgment and the feet of Ammon Ra. Go, and if thy heart be pure, as pure as the garment that thou wearest, and if thy motive be unselfish, thy feet shall not stumble, and thy being shall be filled with light. But remember that Typhon and his hosts of death lurk in every shadow and that death is the result of failure."

Aradamas turned and again folded his arms over his breast in the sign of the cross. As he walked slowly through the somber arch, the shadows of the great Unknown closed over him who had dedicated his life to the search for the Eternal. The priest watched him until he was lost to sight among the massive pillars beyond the span that divided the living from the dead. Then slowly falling on his knees before the gigantic statue of Ra and raising his eyes to the shadows that through the long night concealed the face of the Sun-God, he prayed that the youth might pass from the darkness of the temple pillars to the light he sought.

It seemed that for a second a glow played around the face of the enormous statue and a strange hush of peace filled the ancient temple. The high priest sensed this, for rising, he relighted his lamp and walked slowly away. His beacon of light shone fainter and fainter in the distance, and finally was lost to view among the papyrus blooms of the temple pillars. All that remained were the dying flames on the altar, which sent strange flickering glows over the great stone coffer and the twelve judges of the Egyptian dead.

In the meantime, Aradamas, his hands still crossed on his breast, walked slowly onward and upward until the last ray from the burning altar fire was lost to view among the shadows far behind. Through years of purification he had prepared himself for the great ordeal, and with a purified body and a balanced mind, he moved his way in and out among the pillars that loomed about him. As he walked along, there seemed to radiate from his being a faint golden glow which illuminated the pillars as he passed them. He seemed a ghostly form amid a grove of ancient trees.

Suddenly the pillars widened out to form another vaulted room, dimly lit by a reddish haze. As Aradamas proceeded, there appeared around him swirling wisps of this scarlet light. First they appeared as swiftly moving clouds, but slowly they took form, and strange misty figures in flowing draperies hovered in the air and held out long swaying arms to stay his progress. Wraiths of ruddy mist hovered about him and whispered soft words into his ears, while weird music, like the voice of the storm and the cries of night birds, resounded through the lofty halls. Still Aradamas walked on calm and masterful, his fine, spiritual face outlined by his raven locks in strange contrast to the sinuous forms that gathered around and tried to lure him from his purpose. Unmindful of strange forms that beckoned from ghostly archways and the pleading of soft voices, he passed steadily on his way with but one thought in his mind:

"Fiat Lux!" (Let there be light.)

The ghastly music grew louder and louder, terminating at last in a mighty roar. The very walls shook; the dancing forms swayed like flickering candle shadows and, still pleading and beckoning, vanished among the pillars of the temple.

As the temple walls tottered, Aradamas paused; then with slow measured step he resumed his search for some ray of light, finding always darkness deeper than before. Suddenly before him loomed another doorway, flanked on either side by an obelisk of carved marble, one black and the other white. Through the doorway glowed a dim light, concealed by a gossamer veil of blue silk.

As Aradamas slowly climbed the flight of steps leading to the doorway, there materialized upon the ground at his feet a swirl of lurid mist. In the faint glow that it cast, it twisted like some oily gas, filling the entire chamber with a loathsome miasma. Then out of this cloud issued a gigantic form — half human, half reptile. In its bloodshot eyes burned ruddy pods of demon fire, while great claw-like hands reached out to enfold and crush the slender figure that confronted it. Aradamas wavered for a single instant as the horrible apparition lunged forward, its size doubly magnified in the iridescent fog. Then the white-robed neophyte again slowly advanced, his arms still crossed on his breast. He raised his fine face, illumined by a divine light, and courageously faced the hideous specter. As he confronted the menacing form, for an instant it loomed over him like a towering demon. Suddenly Aradamas raised the cross he carried and held it up before the monster. As he did so, the Crux Ansata gleamed with a wondrous golden light, which, striking the oily, scaly monster, seemed to dissolve its every particle into golden sparks. As the last of the demon guardians vanished before the rays of the cross, a bolt of lightning flashed through the ancient hallways and, striking the veil that hung between the obelisks, rent it down the center and disclosed a vaulted chamber with a circular dome, dimly lighted by invisible lamps.

Bearing his now flaming cross, Aradamas entered the room and instinctively gazed upward to the lofty dome. There, floating in space, far above his head, he saw a great closed eye surrounded by fleecy clouds and rainbow colors. Long Aradamas gazed upon the wonderful sight, for he knew that it was the Eye of Horus, the All-Seeing Eye of the gods.

As he stood there, he prayed that the will of the gods might be made known unto him and that in some way he might be found worthy to open that closed eye in the temple of the living God.

As he stood there gazing upward, the eyelid flickered. As the great orb slowly opened, the chamber was filled with a dazzling, blinding light that seemed to consume the very stones with fire. Aradamas staggered. It seemed as if every atom of his being was scorched by the brilliance of that glow. He instinctively closed his eyes and now he feared to open them, for in that terrific blaze of splendor it seemed that only blindness would follow his action. Little by little, a strange feeling of peace and calm descended upon him and at length he dared to open his eyes to find that the glare was gone, the entire chamber was bathed in a soft, wondrous glow from the mighty Eye in the ceiling. The white robe he had worn had also given place to one of living fire which blazed as though with the reflection of thousands of lesser eyes from the divine orb above. As his eyes became accustomed to the glow, he saw that he was no longer alone. He was surrounded by twelve white-robed figures who, bowing before him, held up strange insignia wrought from living gold.

As Aradamas looked, all the figures pointed, and as he followed the direction of their hands, he saw a staircase of living light that led far up into the dome and passed the Eye in the ceiling.

With one voice, the twelve said: "Yonder lies the way of liberation."

Without a moment's hesitation, Aradamas mounted the staircase, and with feet that seemed to barely touch the steps, climbed upward into the dawn of a great unknown. At last, after climbing many steps, he reached a doorway that opened as he neared it. The breath of morning air fanned his cheek and a golden ray of sunshine played among the waves of his dark hair. He stood on the top of a mighty pyramid, before him a blazing altar. In the distance, far over the horizon, the rolling sands of the Egyptian desert reflected the first rays of the morning sun which, like a globe of golden fire, rose again out of the eternal East. As

Aradamus stood there, a voice that seemed to issue from the very heavens chanted a strange song, and a hand, reaching out as it were from the globe of day itself, placed a serpent wrought of gold upon the brow of the new initiate.

"Behold Khepera, the rising sun! For as he brings the mighty globe of day out of the darkness of night, between his claws, so for thee the Sun of Spirit has risen from the darkness of night and in the name of the living God, we hail thee Priest of Ra."

SO MOTE IT BE

Freemasonic Symbolism
(1928)

IN several early Masonic manuscripts—for example, the Harleian, Sloane, Lansdowne, and Edinburgh-Kilwinning—it is stated that the craft of initiated builders existed before the Deluge, and that its members were employed in the building of the Tower of Babel. A Masonic Constitution dated 1701 gives the following naive account of the origin of the sciences, arts, and crafts from which the major part of Masonic symbolism is derived:

"How this worthy Science was first begunne, I shall tell. Before Noah's Flood, there was a man called Lameck as it is written in the 4 Chap. of Gen.: and this Lameck had two Wives. The one was called Adah, and the other Zillah; by the first wife Adah he gott two Sons, the one called Jaball, and the other Juball, and by the other wife Zillah he got a Son and Daughter, and the four children found the beginning of all Crafts in the world. This Jaball was the elder Son, and he found the Craft of Geometric, and he parted flocks, as of Sheep and Lambs in the fields, and first wrought Houses of Stone and Tree, as it is noted in the Chap, aforesaid, and his Brother Juball found the crafte of Musick, of Songs, Organs and Harp. The Third Brother [Tubal-cain] found out Smith's craft to work Iron and steel, and their sister Naamah found out the art of Weaving. These children did know thatt God would take Vengeance for Sinne, either by fire or water, wherefor they wrote these Sciences which they had found in Two Pillars of stone, thatt they might be found after the Flood. The one stone was called Marbell—cannott burn with Fire, and the other was called Laturus [brass?], thatt cannott drown in the Water." The author of this Constitution there upon declares that one of these pillars was later discovered by Hermes, who communicated to mankind the secrets thereon inscribed.

In his *Antiquities of the Jews,* Josephus writes that Adam had forewarned his descendants that sinful humanity would be destroyed by a deluge. In order to preserve their science and philosophy, the children of Seth therefore raised two pillars, one of brick and the other of stone, on which were inscribed the keys to their knowledge. The Patriarch Enoch—whose name means the Initiator—is evidently a personification of the sun, since he lived 365 years. He also constructed an underground temple consisting of nine vaults, one beneath the other, placing in the deepest vault a triangular tablet of gold bearing upon it the absolute and ineffable Name of Deity. According to some accounts, Enoch made two golden *deltas.* The larger he placed upon the white cubical altar in the lowest vault and the smaller he gave into the keeping of his son, Methuseleh, who did the actual construction work of the brick chambers according to the pattern revealed to his father by the Most High. In the form and arrangement of these vaults Enoch epitomized the nine spheres of the ancient Mysteries and the nine sacred strata of the earth through which the initiate must pass to reach the flaming Spirit dwelling in its central core.

According to Freemasonic symbolism, Enoch, fearing that all knowledge of the sacred Mysteries would be lost at the time of the Deluge, erected the two columns mentioned in the quotation. Upon the metal column in appropriate allegorical symbols he engraved the secret reaching and upon the marble column placed an inscription stating that a short distance away a priceless treasure would be discovered in a subterranean vault. After having thus faithfully completed his labors, Enoch was translated from the brow Of Mount Moriah. In time the location of the secret vaults was lost, but after the lapse of ages there came another builder—an initiate after the order of Enoch—and he, while laying the foundations for another temple to the Great Architect of the Universe, discovered the long-lost vaults and the secrets contained within.

John Leylande was appointed by King Henry VIII to go through the archives of the various religious institutions dissolved by the king and remove for preservation any books or manuscripts of an important character. Among the documents copied by Leylande was a series of questions and answers concerning the mystery of Masonry written by King Henry VI. In answer to the question, "How came Masonry into England?" the document States that Peter Gower, a Grecian, traveled for knowledge in Egypt, Syria, and every land where the Phœnicians had planted Masonry; winning entrance in all lodges of Masons, he learned much, and returning, dwelt in Greater Greece. He became renowned for his wisdom, formed a great lodge at Groton, and made many Masons, some of whom journeyed in France, spreading Masonry there; from France in the course of time the order passed into England.

To even the superficial student of the subject it must be evident that the name of *Peter Gower*, the Grecian, is merely an Anglicized form of *Pythagoras;* consequently Groton, where he formed his lodge, is easily identified with Crotona. A link is thus established between the philosophic Mysteries of Greece and mediæval Freemasonry. In his notes on King Henry's questions and answers, William Preston enlarges upon the vow of secrecy as it was practiced by the ancient initiates. On the authority of Pliny he describes how Anaxarchus, having been imprisoned in order to extort from him some of the secrets with which he had been entrusted, bit out his own tongue and threw it in the face of Nicocreon, the tyrant of Cyprus. Preston adds that the Athenians revered a brazen statue that was represented without a tongue to denote the sanctity with which they regarded their oath-bound secrets. It is also noteworthy that, according to King Henry's manuscript, Masonry had its origin in the East and was the carrier of the arts and sciences of civilization to the primitive humanity of the western nations.

Conspicuous among the symbols of Freemasonry are the seven liberal arts and sciences. By *grammar* man is taught to express in noble and adequate language his innermost thoughts and ideals; by *rhetoric* he is enabled to conceal his ideals under the protecting cover of ambiguous language and figures of speech; by *logic* he is trained in the organization of the intellectual faculties with which he has been endowed; by *arithmetic* he not only is instructed in the mystery of universal order but also gains the key to multitude, magnitude, and proportion; by *geometry* he is inducted into the mathematics of form, the harmony and rhythm of angles, and the philosophy of organization; by *music* he is reminded that the universe is founded upon the laws of celestial harmonics and that harmony and rhythm are all-pervading; by *astronomy* he gains an understanding of the immensities of time and space, of the proper relationship between himself and the universe, and of the awesomeness of that Unknown Power which is driving the countless stars of the firmament through illimitable space. Equipped with the knowledge conferred by familiarity with the liberal arts and sciences, the studious Freemason therefore finds himself confronted by few problems with which he cannot cope.

THE DIONYSIAC ARCHITECTS

The most celebrated of the ancient fraternities of artisans was that of the Dionysiac Architects. This organization was composed exclusively of initiates of the Bacchus-Dionysos cult and was peculiarly consecrated to the science of building and the art of decoration. Acclaimed as being the custodians of a secret and sacred knowledge of architectonics, its members were entrusted with the design and erection of public buildings and monuments. The superlative excellence of their handiwork elevated the members of the guild to a position of surpassing dignity; they were regarded as the master craftsmen of the earth. Because of the first dances held in honor of Dionysos, he was considered the founder and patron of the theater, and the Dionysians specialized in the construction of buildings adapted for the presentation of dramatic performances. In the circular or semicircular orchestra they invariably erected an altar to Æschylus, the famous Greek poet, that while appearing in one of his own plays he was suspected by a mob of angry spectators of revealing one of the profound secrets of the Mysteries and was forced to seek refuge at the altar of Dionysos.

So carefully did the Dionysiac Architects safeguard the secrets of their craft that only fragmentary records exist of their esoteric teachings. John A. Weisse thus sums up the meager data available concerning the order:

"They made their appearance certainly not later than 1000 B.C., and appear to have enjoyed particular privileges and immunities. They also possessed secret means of recognition, and were bound together by special ties only known to themselves. The richer of this fraternity were bound to provide for their poorer brethren. They were divided into communities, governed by a Master and Wardens. They held a grand festival annually, and were held in high esteem. Their ceremonials were regarded as sacred. It has been claimed that Solomon, at the instance of Hiram, King of Tyre, employed them at his temple and palaces. They were also employed at the construction of the Temple of Diana at Ephesus. They had means of intercommunication all over the then known world, and from them, doubtless, sprang the guilds of the Traveling Masons known in the Middle Ages." (See *The Obelisk and Freemasonry.*)

The fraternity of the Dionysiac Architects spread throughout all of Asia Minor, even reaching Egypt and India. They established themselves in nearly all the countries bordering on the Mediterranean, and with the rise of the Roman Empire found their way into Central Europe and even into England. The most stately and enduring buildings in Constantinople, Rhodes, Athens, and Rome were erected by these inspired craftsmen. One of the most illustrious of their number was Vitruvius, the great architect, renowned as the author of *De Architectura Libri Decem.* In the various sections of his book Vitruvius gives several hints as to the philosophy underlying the Dionysiac concept of the principle of symmetry applied to the science of architecture, as derived from a consideration of the proportions established by Nature between the parts and members of the human body. The following extract from Vitruvius on the subject of symmetry is representative:

"The design of a temple depends on symmetry, the principles of which must be most carefully observed by the architect. They are due to proportion. Proportion is a correspondence among the measures of the members of an entire work, and of the whole to a certain part selected as standard. From this result the principles of symmetry. Without symmetry and proportion there can be no principles in the design of any temple; that is, if there is no precise relation between its members, as in the case of those of a well-shaped man. For the human body is so designed by nature that the face, from the chin to the top of the forehead and the lowest roots of the hair, is a tenth part of the whole height; the open hand from the wrist to the tip of the middle finger is just the same; the head from the chin to the crown is an eighth, and with the neck and shoulder from the top of the breast to the lowest roots of the hair is a sixth; from the middle of the breast to the summit of the crown is a fourth. If we take the height of the face itself, the distance from the bottom of the chin to the underside of the nostrils [and from that point] to a line between the eyebrows is the same; from there to the lowest roots of the hair is also a third, comprising the forehead. The length of the foot is one sixth of the height of the body; of the forearm, one fourth; and the breadth of the breast is also one fourth. The other members, too, have their own symmetrical proportions, and it was by employing them that the famous painters and sculptors of antiquity attained to great and endless renown."

The edifices raised by the Dionysiac Builders were indeed "sermons in stone." Though unable to comprehend fully the cosmic principles thus embodied in these masterpieces of human ingenuity and industry, even the uninitiated were invariably overwhelmed by the sense of majesty and symmetry resulting from the perfect coordination of pillars, spans, arches, and domes. By variations in the details of size, material, type, arrangement, ornamentation, and color, these inspired builders believed it possible to provoke in the nature of the onlooker certain distinct mental or emotional reactions. Vitruvius, for example, describes the disposition of bronze vases about a room so as to produce certain definite changes in the tone and quality of the human voice. In like manner, each chamber in the Mysteries through which the candidate passed had its own peculiar acoustics. Thus in one chamber the voice of the priest was amplified until his words caused the very room to vibrate, while in another the voice was diminished and softened to such a degree that it sounded like the distant tinkling of silver bells. Again, in some of the underground passageways the candidate was apparently bereft of the power of speech, for though he shouted at the top of his voice not even a whisper was audible to his ears. After progressing a few feet, however, he would discover that his softest sigh would be reechoed a hundred times.

The supreme ambition of the Dionysiac Architects was the construction of buildings which would create distinct impressions consistent with the purpose for which the structure itself was designed. In common with the Pythagoreans, they believed it possible by combinations of straight lines and curves to induce any desired mental attitude or emotion. They labored, therefore, to the end of producing a building perfectly harmonious with the structure of the universe itself. They may have even believed that an edifice so constructed because it was in no respect at variance with any existing reality would not be subject to dissolution but would endure throughout the span of mortal time. As a logical deduction from their philosophic trend of thought, such a building—*en rapport* with Cosmos—would also have become an oracle. Certain early works on magical philosophy hint that the Ark of the Covenant was oracular in character because of specially prepared chambers in its interior. These by their shape and arrangement were so attuned to the vibrations of the invisible world that they caught and amplified the voices of the ages imprinted upon and eternally existent in the substance of the astral light.

Unskilled in these ancient subtleties of their profession, modern architects often create architectural absurdities which would cause their creators to blush with shame did they comprehend their actual symbolic import. Thus, phallic emblems are strewn in profusion among the adornments of banks, office buildings, and department stores. Christian churches also may be surmounted with Brahmin or Mohammedan domes or be designed in a style suitable for a Jewish synagogue or a Greek temple to Pluto. These incongruities may be considered trivial in importance by the modern designer, but to the trained psychologist the purpose for which a building was erected is frustrated in large measure by the presence of such architectural discordances. Vitruvius thus defines the principle of propriety as conceived and applied by the Dionysians:

"Propriety is that: perfection of style which comes when a work is authoritatively constructed on approved principles. It arises from prescription, from usage, or from nature. From prescription, in the case of hypæthral edifices, open to the sky, in honour of Jupiter Lightning, the Heaven, the Sun, or the Moon: for these are gods whose semblances and manifestations we behold before our very eyes in the sky when it is cloudless and bright. The temples of Minerva, Mars, and Hercules will be Doric, since the virile strength of these gods makes daintiness entirely inappropriate to their houses. In temples to Venus, Flora, Proserpine, Spring-Water, and the Nymphs, the Corinthian order will be found to have peculiar significance, because these are delicate divinities and so its rather slender outlines, its flowers, leaves, and ornamental volutes will lend propriety where it is due. The construction of temples of the Ionic order to Juno, Diana, Father Bacchus, and the other gods of that kind, will be in keeping with the middle position which they hold; for the building of such will be an appropriate combination of the severity of the Doric and the delicacy of the Corinthian."

In describing the societies of Ionian artificers, Joseph Da Costa declares the Dionysiac rites to have been founded upon the science of astronomy, which by the initiates of this order was correlated to the builder's art. In various documents dealing with the origin of architecture are found hints to the effect that the great buildings erected by these initiated craftsmen were based upon geometrical patterns derived from the constellations. Thus, a temple might be planned according to the constellation of Pegasus or a court of judgment modeled after the constellation of the Scales. The Dionysians evolved a peculiar code by which they were able to communicate with one another in the dark and both the symbols and the terminology of their guild were derived, in the main, from the elements of architecture.

While stigmatized as pagans by reason of their philosophic principles, it is noteworthy that these Dionysiac craftsmen were almost universally employed in the erection of early Christian abbeys and cathedrals, whose stones even to this very day bear distinguishing marks and symbols cut into their surfaces by these illustrious builders. Among the ornate carvings upon the fronts of great churches of the Old World are frequently found representations of compasses, squares, rules, mallets, and clusters of builders' tools skillfully incorporated into mural decorations and even placed in the hands of the effigies of saints and prophets standing in exalted niches. A great mystery was contained in the ancient portals of the Cathedral Of Notre Dame which were destroyed during the French Revolution, for among their carvings were numerous Rosicrucian and Masonic emblems; and according to the records preserved by alchemists who studied their bas-reliefs, the secret processes for metallic transmutation were set forth in their grotesque yet most significant figures.

The checkerboard floor upon which the modern Freemasonic lodge stands is the old tracing board of the Dionysiac Architects, and while the modern organization is no longer limited to workmen's guilds it still preserves in its symbols the metaphysical doctrines of the ancient society of which it is presumably the outgrowth. The investigator of the origin of Freemasonic symbolism who desires to trace the development of the order through the ages will find a practical suggestion in the following statement of Charles W. Heckethorn:

"But considering that Freemasonry is a tree the roots of which spread through so many soils, it follows that traces thereof must be found in its fruit; that its language and ritual should retain much of the various sects and institutions it has passed through before arriving at their present state, and in Masonry we meet with Indian, Egyptian, Jewish, and Christian ideas, terms therefrom the supreme ambition of their craft and symbols." (See *The Secret Societies of All Ages and Countries.*)

The Roman *Collegia* of skilled architects were apparently a subdivision of the greater Ionian body, their principles and organization being practically identical with the older Ionian institution. It has been suspected that the Dionysians also profoundly influenced early Islamic culture, for part of their symbolism found its way into the Mysteries of the dervishes. At one time the Dionysians referred to themselves as Sons of Solomon, and one of the most important of their symbols was the Seal of Solomon—two interlaced triangles. This motif is frequently seen in conspicuous parts of Mohammedan mosques. The Knights Templars—who were suspected of anything and everything—are believed to have contacted these Dionysiac artificers and to have introduced many of their symbols and doctrines into mediæval Europe. But Freemasonry most of all owes to the Dionysiac cult the great mass of its symbols and rituals which are related to the science of architecture. From these ancient and illustrious artisans it also received the legacy of the unfinished Temple of Civilization-that vast, invisible structure upon which these initiated builders have labored continuously since the inception of their fraternity. This mighty edifice, which has fallen and been rebuilt time after time but whose foundations remain unmoved, is the true Everlasting House of which the temple on the brow of Mount Moriah was but an impermanent symbol.

Aside from the operative aspect of their order, the Dionysiac Architects had a speculative philosophic code. Human society they considered as a rough and untrued ashlar but lately chiseled from the quarry of elemental Nature. This crude block was the true object upon which these skilled craftsmen labored—polishing it, squaring it, and with the aid of fine carvings transforming it into a miracle of beauty. While mystics released their souls from the bondage of matter by meditation and philosophers found their keenest joy in the profundities of thought, these master workmen achieved liberation from the Wheel of Life and Death by learning to swing their hammers with the same rhythm that moves the swirling forces of Cosmos. They venerated the Deity under the guise of a Great Architect and Master Craftsman who was ever gouging rough ashlars from the fields of space and truing them into universes. The Dionysians affirmed constructiveness to be the supreme expression of the soul, and attuning themselves with the ever-visible constructive natural processes going on around them, believed immortality could be achieved by thus becoming a part of the creative agencies of Nature.

Solomon, The Personification Of Universal Wisdom

The name Solomon may be divided into three syllables, SOL-OM-ON, symbolizing light, glory, and truth collectively and respectively. The Temple of Solomon is, therefore, first of all "the House of Everlasting Light," its earthly symbol being the temple of stone on the brow of Mount Moriah. According to the Mystery teachings, there are three Temples of Solomon—as there are three Grand Masters, three Witnesses, and three Tabernacles of the Transfiguration. The first temple is the Grand House of the Universe, in the midst of which sits the sun (SOL) upon his golden throne. The twelve signs of the zodiac as Fellow-Craftsmen gather around their shining lord. Three lights—the stellar, the solar, and the lunar—illuminate this Cosmic Temple. Accompanied by his retinue of planets, moons, and asteroids, this Divine King (SOLomon), whose glory no earthly monarch shall ever equal, passes in stately pomp down the avenues of space. Whereas *CHiram* represents the active physical light of the sun, SOLomon signifies its invisible but all-powerful, spiritual and intellectual effulgency.

The second symbolic temple is the human body—the Little House made in the image of the Great Universal House.

"Know ye not," asked the Apostle Paul, "that ye are the temple of God, and that the Spirit of God dwelleth in you?" Freemasonry within a temple of stone cannot be other than speculative, but Freemasonry within the living temple of the body is operative. The third symbolic temple is the *Soul*ar House, an invisible structure, the comprehension of which is a supreme Freemasonic arcanum. The mystery of this intangible edifice is concealed under the allegory of the *Soma Psuchicon*, or Wedding Garment described by St. Paul, the Robes of Glory of the High Priest of Israel, the Yellow Robe of the Buddhist monk, and the Robe of Blue and Gold to which Albert Pike refers in his *Symbolism*. The soul, constructed from an invisible fiery substance, a flaming golden metal, is cast by the Master Workman, CHiram Abiff, into the mold of clay (the physical body) and is called the Molten Sea. The temple of the human soul is built by three Master Masons personifying Wisdom, Love, and Service, and when constructed according to the Law of Life the spirit of God dwells in the Holy Place thereof. The *Soul*ar Temple is the true Everlasting House, and he who can *raise* or *cast* it is a Master Mason *indeed!* The best-informed Masonic writers have realized that Solomon's Temple is a representation in miniature of the Universal Temple. Concerning this point, A. E. Waite, in *A New Encyclopædia of Freemasonry*, writes: "It is macrocosmic in character, so that the Temple is a symbol of the universe, a type of manifestation itself."

Solomon, the Spirit of Universal Illumination—mental, spiritual, moral, and physical—is personified in the king of an earthly nation. While a great ruler by that name may have built a temple, he who considers the story solely from its historical angle will never clear away the rubbish that covers the secret vaults. The *rubbish* is interpolated matter in the form of superficial symbols, allegories, and degrees which have no legitimate part in the original Freemasonic Mysteries. Concerning the loss of the true esoteric key to Masonic secrets, Albert Pike writes:

"No one journeys now 'from the high place of Cabaon to the threshing floor of Oman the Yebusite,' nor has seen, 'his Master, clothed in blue and gold;' nor are apprentices and

Fellow-crafts any longer paid at their respective Columns; nor is the Master's working tool the Tracing Board, nor does he use in his work 'Chalk, Charcoal, and an Earthen Vessel,' nor does the Apprentice, becoming a Fellow Craft, pass from the square to the compass; for the meanings of these phrases as symbols have long been lost."

According to the ancient Rabbins, Solomon was an initiate of the Mystery schools and the temple which he built was actually a house of initiation containing amass of pagan philosophic and phallic emblems. The pomegranates, the palm-headed columns, the Pillars before the door, the Babylonian cherubim, and the arrangement of the chambers and draperies all indicate the temple to have been patterned after the sanctuaries of Egypt and Atlantis. Isaac Myer, in *The Qabbalah*, makes the following observation:

"The pseudo-Clement of Rome, writes: 'God made man male and female. The male is Christ: the female, the Church.' The Qabbalists called the Holy Spirit, the mother, and the Church of Israel, the Daughter. Solomon engraved on the walls of his Temple, likenesses of the male and female principles, to adumbrate this mystery; such, it is said, were the figures of the cherubim. This was, however, not in obedience to the words of the Thorah. They were symbolical of the Upper, the spiritual, the former or maker, positive or male, and the Lower, the passive, the negative or female, formed or made by the first."

Masonry came to Northern Africa and Asia Minor from the lost continent of Atlantis, not under its present name but rather under the general designation Sun and Fire Worship. The ancient Mysteries did not cease to exist when Christianity became the world's most powerful religion. Great Pan did not die! Freemasonry is the proof of his survival. The pre-Christian Mysteries simply assumed the symbolism of the new faith, perpetuating through its emblems and allegories the same truths which had been the property of the wise since the beginning of the world. There is no true explanation, therefore, for Christian symbols save that which is concealed within pagan philosophy.

Without the mysterious keys carried by the hierophants of the Egyptian, Brahmin, and Persian cults the gates of Wisdom cannot be opened. Consider with reverent spirit, therefore, the sublime allegory of the Temple and its Builders, realizing that beneath its literal interpretation lies hidden a Royal Secret.

According to the Talmudic legends, Solomon understood the mysteries of the Qabbalah. He was also an alchemist and a necromancer, being able to control the demons, and from them and other inhabitants of the invisible worlds he secured much of his wisdom. In his translation of *Clavicula Salomonis,* or *The Key of Solomon the King,* a work presumably setting forth the magical secrets gathered by Solomon and used by him in the conjuration of spirits and which, according to Frank C. Higgins, contains many sidelights on Masonic initiatory rituals, S. L. MacGregor-Mathers recognizes the probability that King Solomon was a magician in the fullest sense of that word. "I see no reason to doubt," he affirms, "the tradition which assigns the authorship of the 'Key' to King Solomon, for among others Josephus, the Jewish historian, especially mentions the magical works attributed to that monarch; this is confirmed by many Eastern traditions, and his magical skill is frequently mentioned in the Arabian Nights."

Concerning Solomon's supernatural powers, Josephus writes in his *Eighth Book of the Antiquities of the Jews:*

"Now the sagacity and wisdom which God had bestowed on Solomon was so great that he exceeded the ancients, in so much that he was no way inferior to the Egyptians, who are said to have been beyond all men in understanding; [...] God also enabled him to learn that skill which expelled demons, which is a science useful and sanative to him. He composed such incantations also by which distempers are alleviated. And he left behind him the manner of using exorcisms, by which they drive away demons, so that they never return; and this method of cure is of great force unto this day."

The mediæval alchemists were convinced that King Solomon understood the secret processes of Hermes by means of which it was possible to multiply metals. Dr. Bacstrom writes that the *Universal Spirit* (CHiram) assisted King Solomon to build his temple, because Solomon being wise in the wisdom of alchemy knew how to control this incorporeal essence and, setting it to work for him, caused the invisible universe to supply him with vast amounts of gold and silver which most people believed were mined by natural methods.

The mysteries of the Islamic faith are now in the keeping of the dervishes—men who, renouncing worldliness, have withstood the test of a thousand and one days of temptation. Jelal-ud-din, the great Persian Sufic poet and philosopher, is accredited with having founded the Order of Mevlevi, or the "dancing dervishes," whose movements exoterically signify the motions of the celestial bodies and esoterically result in the establishment of a rhythm which stimulates the centers of spiritual consciousness within the dancer's body.

"According to the mystical canon, there are always on earth a certain number of holy men who are admitted to intimate communion with the Deity. The one who occupies the highest position among his contemporaries is called the 'Axis' (Qûtb) or 'Pole' of his time. [...] Subordinate to the Qûtb are two holy beings who bear the title of 'The Faithful Ones,' and are assigned places on his right and left respectively. Below these is a quartette of 'Intermediate Ones' (Evtâd); and on successively lower planes ate five 'Lights' (Envâr), and seven 'Very Good' (Akhyâr). The next rank is filled by forty 'Absent Ones' (Rijal-i-ghaib), also termed 'Martyrs' (Shuheda). When an 'Axis' quits this earthly existence, he is succeeded by the 'Faithful One' who has occupied the place at his right hand. [...] For to these holy men, who also bear the collective titles of 'Lords of Souls,' and 'Directors,' is committed a spiritual supremacy over mankind far exceeding the temporal authority of earthly rulers." (See *Mysticism and Magic in Turkey*, by L. M. J. Garnett.)

The *Axis* is a mysterious individual who, unknown and unsuspected, mingles with mankind and who, according to tradition, has his favorite seat upon the roof of the Caaba. J. P.

Brown, in *The Dervishes,* gives a description of these "Master Souls."

FREEMASONRY'S PRICELESS HERITAGE

The *sanctum sanctorum* of Freemasonry is ornamented with the gnostic jewels of a thousand ages; its rituals ring with the divinely inspired words of seers and sages. A hundred religious have brought their gifts of wisdom to its altar; arts and sciences unnumbered have contributed to its symbolism. Freemasonry is a world-wide university, teaching the liberal arts and sciences of the soul to all who will hearken to its words. Its chairs are seats of learning and its pillars uphold an arch of universal education. Its trestleboards are inscribed with the eternal verities of all ages and upon those who comprehend its sacred depths has dawned the realization that within the Freemasonic Mysteries lie hidden the long-lost arcana sought by all peoples since the genesis of human reason.

Though the temples of Thebes and Karnak be now but majestic heaps of broken and time-battered stone, the spirit: of Egyptian philosophy still marches triumphant through the centuries. Though the rock-hewn sanctuaries of the ancient Brahmins be now deserted and their carvings crumbled into dust, still the wisdom of the Vedas endures. Though the oracles be silenced and the House of the Mysteries be now but rows of ghostly columns, still shines the spiritual glory of Hellas with luster undiminished. Though Zoroaster, Hermes, Pythagoras, Plato, and Aristotle are now but dim memories in a world once rocked by the transcendency of their intellectual genius, still in the mystic temple of Freemasonry these god-men live again in their words and symbols; and the candidate, passing through the initiations, feels himself face to face with these illumined hierophants of days long past.

The Fraternity of the Rose Cross
(1928)

WHO were the Rosicrucians? Were they an organization of profound thinkers rebelling against the inquisitional religious and philosophical limitations of their time or were they isolated transcendentalists united only by the similarity of their viewpoints and deductions? Where was the "House of the Holy Spirit, "in which, according to their manifestoes, they met once a year to plan the future activities of their Order? Who was the mysterious person referred to as "Our Illustrious Father and Brother C.R.C."? Did those three letters actually stand for the words "Christian Rosie Cross"? Was Christian Rosencreutz, the supposed author of the *Chymical Nuptials*, the same person who with three others founded "The Society of the Rose Cross"?

What relationship existed between Rosicrucianism and mediæval Freemasonry? Why were the destinies of these two organizations so closely interwoven? Is the "Brotherhood of the Rose Cross" the much-sought-after link connecting the Freemasonry of the Middle Ages with the symbolism and mysticism of antiquity, and are its secrets being perpetuated by modern Masonry? Did the original Rosicrucian Order disintegrate in the latter part of the eighteenth century, or does the Society still exist as an organization, maintaining the same secrecy for which it was originally famous?

What was the true purpose for which the "Brotherhood of the Rose Cross" was formed? Were the Rosicrucians a religious and philosophic brotherhood, as they claimed to be, or were their avowed tenets a blind to conceal the true object of the

Fraternity, which possibly was the political control of Europe? These are some of the problems involved in the study of Rosicrucianism.

There are four distinct theories regarding the Rosicrucian enigma. Each is the result of a careful consideration of the evidence by scholars who have spent their lives ransacking the archives of Hermetic lore. The conclusions reached demonstrate clearly the inadequacy of the records available concerning the genesis and early activities of the "Brethren of the Rose Cross."

THE FIRST POSTULATE

It is assumed that the Rosicrucian Order existed historically in accordance with the description of its foundation and subsequent activities published in its manifesto, the *Fama Fraternitatis*, which is believed to have been written in the year 1610, but apparently did not appear in print until 1614, although an earlier edition is suspected by some authorities. Intelligent consideration of the origin of Rosicrucianism requires a familiarity with the contents of the first and most important of its documents. The *Fama Fraternitatis* begins with a reminder to all the world of God's goodness and mercy, and it warns the intelligentsia that their egotism and covetousness cause them to follow after false prophets and to ignore the true knowledge which God in His goodness has revealed to them. Hence, a reformation is necessary, and God has raised up philosophers and sages for this purpose.

In order to assist in bringing about the reformation, a mysterious person called "The Highly Illuminated Father C.R.C.," a German by birth, descended of a noble family, but himself a poor man, instituted the "Secret Society of the Rose Cross." C.R.C. was placed in a cloister when only five years of age, but later becoming dissatisfied with its educational system, he associated himself with a brother of Holy Orders who was setting forth on a pilgrimage to the Holy Land. They started out together, but the brother died at Cyprus and C.R.C! continued alone to

Damascus. Poor health prevented him from reaching Jerusalem, so he remained at Damascus, studying with the philosophers who dwelt there.

While pursuing his studies, he heard of a group of mystics and Qabbalists abiding in the mystic Arabian city of Damcar. Giving up his desire to visit Jerusalem, he arranged with the Arabians for his transportation to Damcar. C.R.C. was but sixteen years of age when he arrived at Damcar. He was received as one who had been long expected, a comrade and a friend in philosophy, and was instructed in the secrets of the Arabian adepts. While there, C.R.C. learned the Arabic tongue and translated the sacred book *M* into Latin; and upon returning to Europe he brought this important volume with him.

After studying three years in Damcar, C.R.C. departed for the city of Fez, where the Arabian magicians declared further information would be given him. At Fez he was instructed how to communicate with the Elementary inhabitants [probably the Nature spirits], and these disclosed to him many other great secrets of Nature. While the philosophers in Fez were not so great as those in Damcar, the previous experiences of C.R.C. enabled him to distinguish the true from the false and thus add greatly to his store of knowledge.

After two years in Fez, C.R.C. sailed for Spain, carrying with him many treasures, among them rare plants and animals accumulated during his wanderings. He fondly hoped that the learned men of Europe would receive with gratitude the rare intellectual and material treasures which he had brought for their consideration. Instead he encountered only ridicule, for the so-called wise were afraid to admit their previous ignorance lest their prestige be impaired. At this point in the narrative is an interpolation stating that Paracelsus, while not a member of the "Fraternity of the Rose Cross," had read the book *M* and from a consideration of its contents had secured information which made him the foremost physician of mediæval Europe.

Tired, but not discouraged, as the result of the fruitlessness of his efforts, C.R.C. returned to Germany, where he built a house in which he could quietly carry on his study and research. He also manufactured a number of rare scientific instruments for research purposes. While he could have made himself famous had he cared to commercialize his knowledge, he preferred the companionship of God to the esteem of men.

After five years of retirement, he decided to renew his struggle for a reformation of the arts and sciences of his day, this time with the aid of a few trusted friends. He sent to the cloister where his early training had been received and called to himself three brethren, whom he bound by an oath to preserve inviolate the secrets he should impart and to write down for the sake of posterity the information.

When the first of the Order died in England, it was decided that the burial places of the members should be secret. Soon afterward Father C.R.C. called the remaining six together, and it is supposed that then he prepared his own symbolic tomb. The Fama records that none of the Brothers alive at the time of its writing knew when Father C.R.C. died or where he was buried. His body was accidentally discovered 120 years after his death when one of the Brothers, who possessed considerable architectural skill, decided to make some alterations in the "House of the Holy Spirit." [It is only suspected that the tomb was in this building.]

While making his alterations, the Brother discovered a memorial tablet upon which were inscribed the names of the early members of the Order. This he decided to transfer to a more imposing chapel, for at that time no one knew in what country Father C.R.C. had died, this information having been concealed by the original members. In attempting to remove the memorial tablet, which was held in place by a large nail, some stones and plastering were broken from the wall, disclosing a door concealed in the masonry. The members of the Order immediately cleared away the rest of the débris and uncovered the entrance to a vault. Upon the door in large letters were the words: POST CXX ANNOS PATEBO. This, according to the mystic interpretation of the Brethren, meant, "In 120 years I shall come forth."

The following morning the door was opened and the members entered a vault with seven sides and seven corners, each side five feet broad and eight feet high. Although the sun never penetrated this tomb, it was brilliantly illuminated by a mysterious light in the ceiling. In the center was a circular altar, upon which were brass plates engraved with strange characters. In each of the seven sides was a small door which, upon being opened, revealed a number of boxes filled with books, secret instructions, and the supposedly lost arcanum of the Fraternity.

Upon moving the altar to one side a brass cover was disclosed. Lifting this revealed a body, presumedly that of C.R.C., which, although it had lain there 120 years, was as well preserved as though it had just been interred. It was ornamented and attired in the robes of the Order, and in one hand was clasped a mysterious parchment which, next to the Bible, was the most valued possession of the Society. After thoroughly investigating the contents of the secret chamber, the brass plate and altar were put back in place, the door of the vault was again sealed, and the Brothers went their respective ways, their spirits raised and their faith increased by the miraculous spectacle which they had beheld.

The document ends by saying in effect, "In accordance with the will of Father C.R.C., the *Fama* has been prepared and sent forth to the wise and learned of all Europe in five languages, that all may know and understand the secrets of the august Fraternity. All of sincere soul who labor for the glory of God are invited to communicate with the Brethren and are promised that their appeal shall be heard, regardless of where they are or how the messages are sent. At the same time, those of selfish and ulterior motives are warned that only sorrow and misery will attend any who attempt to discover the Fraternity without a clean heart and a pure mind."

Such, in brief, is the story of the *Fama Fraternitatis.* Those who accept it literally regard Father C.R.C. as the actual founder of the Brotherhood, which he is believed to have organized about 1400. The fact that historical corroboration of the important points of the Fama has never been discovered is held against this theory. There is no proof that Father C.R.C. ever approached the learned men of Spain. The mysterious city of Damcar cannot be found, and there is no record that anywhere in Germany there existed a place where great numbers of the halt and sick came and were mysteriously healed. A. E. Waite's *The Secret Tradition in Freemasonry* contains a picture of Father C.R.C. showing him with a long beard upon his breast, sitting before a table upon which burns a candle. One hand is supporting his head, and the other is resting the tip of its index finger on the temple of a human skull. The picture, however (see plate at head of chapter), proves nothing. Father C.R.C. was never seen by other than members of his own Order, and they did not preserve a description of him. That his name was Christian Rosencreutz is most improbable, as the two were not even associated until the writing of the *Chymical Nuptials*.

THE SECOND POSTULATE

Those Masonic brethren who have investigated the subject accept the historical existence of the "Brotherhood of the Rose Cross" but are divided concerning the origin of the Order. One group holds the society originated in mediæval Europe as an outgrowth of alchemical speculation. Robert Macoy, 33°, believes that Johann Valentin Andreæ, a German theologian, was the true founder, and he also believes it possible that this divine merely reformed and amplified an existing society which had been founded by Sir Henry Cornelius Agrippa. Some believe that Rosicrucianism represented the first European invasion of Buddhist and Brahmin culture. Still others hold the opinion that the "Society of the Rose Cross" was founded in Egypt during n the philosophic supremacy of that empire, and that it also perpetuated the Mysteries of ancient Persia and Chaldea.

In his *Anacalypsis,* Godfrey Higgins writes: "The Rosicrucians of Germany are quite ignorant of their origin; but, by tradition, they suppose themselves descendants of the ancient Egyptians, Chaldeans, Magi, and Gymnosophists." (The last was a name given by the followers of Alexander the Great to a caste of naked Wise Men whom they found meditating along the riverbanks in India.) The consensus among these factions is that the story of Father C.R.C., like the Masonic legend of Hiram Abiff, is an allegory and should not be considered literally. A similar problem has confronted students of the Bible, who have found not only difficult, but in the majority of cases impossible, their efforts to substantiate the historical interpretation of the Scriptures.

Admitting the existence of the Rosicrucians as a secret society with both philosophic and political ends, it is remarkable that an organization with members in all parts of Europe could maintain absolute secrecy throughout the centuries. Nevertheless, the "Brothers of the Rose Cross" were apparently able to accomplish this. A great number of scholars and philosophers, among them Sir Francis Bacon and Wolfgang von Goethe, have been suspected of affiliation with the Order, but their connection has not been established to the satisfaction of prosaic historians. Pseudo-Rosicrucians abounded, but the true members of the "Ancient and Secret Order of The Unknown Philosophers" have successfully lived up to their name; to this day they remain unknown.

During the Middle Ages a number of tracts appeared, purporting to be from the pens of Rosicrucians. Many of them, however, were spurious, being issued for their self-aggrandizement by unscrupulous persons who used the revered and magic name Rosicrucian in the hope of gaining religious or political power. This has greatly complicated the work of investigating the Society. One group of pseudo-Rosicrucians went so far as to supply its members with a black cord by which they were to know each other, and warned them that if they broke their vow of secrecy the cord would be used to strangle them. Few of the principles of Rosicrucianism have been preserved in literature, for the original Fraternity published only fragmentary accounts of its principles and activities.

Freemasons and Rosicrucians
The Enlightened

In his *Secret Symbols of the Rosicrucians*, Dr. Franz Hartmann describes the Fraternity as "A secret society of men possessing superhuman—if not supernatural—powers; they were said to be able to prophesy future events, to penetrate into the deepest mysteries of Nature, to transform Iron, Copper, Lead, or Mercury into Gold, to prepare an *Elixir of Life*, or *Universal Panacea*, by the use of which they could preserve their youth and manhood; and moreover it was believed that they could command the *Elemental Spirits of Nature*, and knew the secret of the *Philosopher's Stone*, a substance which rendered him who possessed it all-powerful, immortal, and supremely wise."

The same author further defines a Rosicrucian as "A person who by the process of spiritual awakening has attained a *practical knowledge* of the secret significance of the *Rose* and the *Cross*. * * * To call a person a Rosicrucian does not make him one, nor does the act of calling a person a Christian make him a Christ. The real Rosicrucian or Mason cannot be made; he must grow to be one by the expansion and unfoldment of the divine power within his own heart. The inattention to this truth is the cause that many churches and secret societies are far from being that which their names express."

The symbolic principles of Rosicrucianism are so profound that even today they are little appreciated. Their charts and diagrams are concerned with weighty cosmic principles which they treat with a philosophic understanding decidedly refreshing when compared with the orthodox narrowness prevalent in their day. According to the available records, the Rosicrucians were bound together by mutual aspirations rather than by the laws of a fraternity. The "Brothers of the Rose Cross" are believed to have lived unobtrusively, laboring industriously in trades and professions, disclosing their secret affiliation to no one—in many cases not even to their own families. After the death of C.R.C., most of the Brethren apparently had no central meeting place. Whatever initiatory ritual the Order possessed was so closely guarded that it has never been revealed. Doubtless it was couched in chemical terminology.

Efforts to join the Order were apparently futile, for the Rosicrucians always chose their disciples. Having agreed on one who they believed would do honor to their illustrious fraternity, they communicated with him in one of many mysterious ways. He might receive a letter, either anonymous or with a peculiar seal, usually bearing the letters "C.R.C. "or "R.C. "upon it. He would be instructed to go to a certain place at an appointed time. What was disclosed to him he never revealed, although in many cases his later writings showed that a new influence had come into his life, deepening his understanding and broadening his intellect. A few have written allegorically concerning what they beheld when in the august presence of the "Brethren of the Rose Cross."

Alchemists were sometimes visited in their laboratories by mysterious strangers, who delivered learned discourses concerning the secret processes of the Hermetic arts and, after disclosing certain processes, departed, leaving no trace. Others declared that the "Brothers of the Rose Cross" communicated with them through dreams and visions, revealing the secrets of Hermetic wisdom to them while they were asleep. Having been instructed, the candidate was bound to secrecy not only concerning the chemical formulæ which had been disclosed to him but also concerning the method by which he had secured them. While these nameless adepts were suspected of being "Brothers of the Rose Cross," it could never be proved who they were, and those visited could only conjecture.

Many suspect the Rosicrucian rose to be a conventionalization of the Egyptian and Hindu lotus blossom, with the same symbolic meaning as this more ancient symbol. The *Divine Comedy* stamps Dante Alighieri as being familiar with the theory of Rosicrucianism. Concerning this point, Albert Pike in his *Morals and Dogma* makes this significant statement: "His Hell is but a negative Purgatory. His heaven is composed of a series of Kabalistic circles, divided by a cross, like the Pantacle of Ezekiel. In the center of this cross blooms a rose, and we see the symbol of the Adepts of the Rose-Croix for the first time publicly expounded and almost categorically explained."

Freemasons and Rosicrucians
The Enlightened

Doubt has always existed as to whether the name Rosicrucian came from the symbol of the rose and cross, or whether this was merely a blind to deceive the uninformed and further conceal the true meaning of the Order. Godfrey Higgins believes that the word *Rosicrucian* is not derived from the flower but from the word *Ros,* which means dew. It is also interesting to note that the word *Ras* means wisdom, while *Rus* is translated concealment. Doubtless all of these meanings have contributed to Rosicrucian symbolism.

A. E. Waite holds with Godfrey Higgins that the process of forming the Philosopher's Stone with the aid of dew is the secret concealed within the name Rosicrucian. It is possible that the dew referred to is a mysterious substance within the human brain, closely resembling the description given by alchemists of the dew which, falling from heaven, redeemed the earth. The cross is symbolic of the human body, and the two symbols together—the rose on the cross—signify that the soul of man is crucified upon the body, where it is held by three nails.

It is probable that Rosicrucian symbolism is a perpetuation of the secret tenets of the Egyptian Hermes, and that the Society of Unknown Philosophers is the true link connecting modern Masonry, with its mass of symbols, to ancient Egyptian Hermeticism, the source of that symbolism. In his *Doctrine and Literature of the Kabalah,* A. E. Waite makes this important observation: "There are certain indications which point to a possible connection between Masonry and Rosicrucianism, and this, if admitted, would constitute the first link in its connection with the past. The evidence is, however, inconclusive, or at least unextracted. Freemasonry per se, in spite of the affinity with mysticism which I have just mentioned, has never exhibited any mystic character, nor has it a clear notion how it came by its symbols."

Many of those connected with the development of Freemasonry were suspected of being Rosicrucians; some, as in the case of Robert Fludd, even wrote defenses of this organization. Frank C. Higgins, a modern Masonic symbolist, writes: "Doctor Ashmole, a member of this fraternity [Rosicrucian], is revered by Masons as one of the founders of the first Grand Lodge in London." (See *Ancient Freemasonry.*) Elias Ashmole is but one of many intellectual links connecting Rosicrucianism with the genesis of Freemasonry. The *Encyclopædia Britannica* notes that Elias Ashmole was initiated into the Freemasonic Order in 1646, and further states that he was "the first gentleman, or amateur, to be 'accepted'."

On this same subject, Papus, in his *Tarot of the Bohemians*, has written: "We must not forget that the Rosicrucians were the Initiators of Leibnitz, and the founders of actual Freemasonry through Ashmole." If the founders of Freemasonry were initiated into the Great Arcanum of Egypt—and the symbolism of modern Masonry would indicate that such was the case—then it is reasonable to suppose that they secured their information from a society whose existence they admitted and which was duly qualified to teach them these symbols and allegories.

One theory concerning the two Orders is to the effect that Freemasonry was an outgrowth of Rosicrucianism; in other words, that the "Unknown Philosophers" became known through an organization which they created to serve them in the material world. The story goes on to relate that the Rosicrucian adepts became dissatisfied with their progeny and silently withdrew from the Masonic hierarchy, leaving behind their symbolism and allegories, but carrying away the keys by which the locked symbols could be made to give tip their secret meanings. Speculators have gone so far as to state that, in their opinion, modern Freemasonry has completely absorbed Rosicrucianism and succeeded it as the world's greatest secret society. Other minds of equal learning declare that the Rosicrucian Brotherhood still exists, preserving its individuality as the result of having withdrawn from the Masonic Order.

According to a widely accepted tradition, the headquarters of the Rosicrucian Order is near Carlsbad, in Austria (see Doctor Franz Hartmann). Another version has it that a mysterious school, resembling in general principles the Rosicrucian Fraternity, which calls itself "The Bohemian Brothers," still maintains its individuality in the *Schwarzwald* (Black Forest) of Germany. One thing is certain: with the rise of Freemasonry, the Rosicrucian Order in Europe practically disappeared, and notwithstanding existing statements to the contrary, it is certain that the 18th degree (commonly known as the Rose-Croix) perpetuates many of the symbols of the Rosicrucian Fire Alchemists.

In an anonymous unpublished manuscript of the eighteenth century bearing the earmarks of Rosicrucian Qabbalism appears this statement: "Yet will I now give the over-wise world a paradox to be solved, namely, that some illuminated men have undertaken to found Schools of Wisdom in Europe and these for some peculiar reason have called themselves *Fratres Rosa: Crucis*. But soon afterwards came false schools into existence and corrupted the good intentions of these wise men. Therefore, the Order no longer exists as most people would understand existence, and as this Fraternity of the *Seculo Fili* call themselves *Brothers of the Rosie Cross*, so also will they in the *Seculo Spiritus Sancti* call themselves *Brothers of the Lily Cross* and the *Knights of the White Lion*. Then will the Schools of Wisdom begin again to blossom, but why the first one chose their name and why the others shall also choose theirs, only those can solve who have understanding grounded in Nature."

Political aspirations of the Rosicrucians were expressed through the activities of Sir Francis Bacon, the Comte de St.-Germain, and the Comte di Cagliostro. The last named is suspected of having been an emissary of the Knights Templars, a society deeply involved in transcendentalism, as Eliphas Levi has noted. There is a popular supposition to the effect that the Rosicrucians were at least partial instigators of the French Revolution. (Note particularly the introduction to Lord Bulwer-Lytton's Rosicrucian novel *Zanoni*.)

The Third Postulate

The third theory takes the form of a sweeping denial of Rosicrucianism, asserting that the so-called original Order never had any foundation in fact but was entirely a product of imagination. This viewpoint is best expressed by a number of questions which are still being asked by investigators of this elusive group of metaphysicians. Was the "Brotherhood of the Rose Cross" merely a mythical institution created in the fertile mind of some literary cynic for the purpose of deriding the alchemical and Hermetic sciences? Did the "House of the Holy Spirit" ever exist outside the imagination of some mediæval mystic? Was the whole Rosicrucian story a satire to ridicule the gullibility of scholastic Europe? Was the mysterious Father C.R.C. a product of the literary genius of Johann Valentin Andreæ, or another of similar mind, who, attempting to score alchemical and Hermetic philosophy, unwittingly became a great power in furthering the cause of its promulgation? That at least one of the early documents of the Rosicrucians was from the pen of Andreæ there is little doubt, but for just what purpose he compiled it still remains a matter of speculation. Did Andreæ himself receive from some unknown person, or persons, instructions to be carried out? If he wrote the *Chymical Nuptials of Christian Rosencreutz* when only fifteen years old, was he overshadowed in the preparation of that book?

To these vital questions no answers are forthcoming. A number of persons accepted the magnificent imposture of Andreæ as absolute truth. It is maintained by many that, as a consequence, numerous pseudo-societies sprang up, each asserting that it was the organization concerning which the *Fama Fraternitatis* and the *Confessio Fraternitatis* were written. Beyond doubt there are many spurious orders in existence today; but few of them can offer valid claims that their history dates back farther than the beginning of the nineteenth century.

The mystery associated with the Rosicrucian Fraternity has resulted in endless controversy. Many able minds, notable among them Eugenius Philalethes, Michael Maier, John Heydon, and Robert Fludd, defended the concrete existence of "The Society of Unknown Philosophers." Others equally qualified have asserted it to be of fraudulent origin and doubtful existence. Eugenius Philalethes, while dedicating books to the Order, and himself writing an extended exposition of its principles, disclaims all personal connection with it. Many others have done likewise.

Some are of the opinion that Sir Francis Bacon had a hand in the writing of the *Fama* and *Confessio Fraternitatis,* on the basis that the rhetorical style of these works is similar to that of Bacon's *New Atlantis.* They also contend that certain statements in the latter work point to an acquaintance with Rosicrucian symbology. The elusiveness of the Rosicrucians has caused them to be favorite subject's for literary works. Outstanding among the romances which have been woven around them is *Zanoni.* The author, Lord Bulwer-Lytton, is regarded by some as a member of the Order, while others assert that he applied for membership but was rejected. Pope's *Rape of the Lock,* &c. *Comte de Gabalis* by Abbé de Villars, and essays by De Quincy, Hartmann, Jennings, Mackenzie, and others, are examples of Rosicrucian literature. Although the existence of these mediæval Rosicrucians is difficult to prove, sufficient evidence is at hand to make it extremely probable that there existed in Germany, and afterwards in France, Italy, England, and other European countries, a secret society of illuminated savants who made contributions of great import to the sum of human knowledge, while maintaining absolute secrecy concerning their personalities and their organization.

THE FOURTH POSTULATE

The apparent incongruities of the Rosicrucian controversy have also been accounted for by a purely transcendental explanation. There is evidence that early writers were acquainted with such a supposition—which, however, was popularized only after it had been espoused by Theosophy. This theory asserts that the Rosicrucians actually possessed all the supernatural powers with which they were credited; that they were in reality citizens of two worlds: that, while they had physical bodies for expression on the material plane, they were also capable, through the instructions they received from the Brotherhood, of functioning in a mysterious ethereal body not subject to the limitations of time or distance. By means of this "astral form" they were able to function in the invisible realm of Nature, and in this realm, beyond reach of the profane, their temple was located.

According to this viewpoint, the true Rosicrucian Brotherhood consisted of a limited number of highly developed adepts, or initiates, those of the higher degrees being no longer subject to the laws of mortality; candidates were accepted into the Order only after long periods of probation; adepts possessed the secret of the Philosopher's Stone and knew the process of transmuting the base metals into gold, but taught that these were only allegorical terms concealing the true mystery of human regeneration through the transmutation of the "base elements" of man's lower nature into the "gold" of intellectual and spiritual realization. According to this theory, those who have sought to record the events of importance in connection with the Rosicrucian controversy have invariably failed because they approached their subject from a purely physical or materialistic angle.

These adepts were believed to have been able to teach man how to function away from his physical body at will by assisting him to remove the "rose from the cross." They taught that the spiritual nature was attached to the material form at certain points, symbolized by the "nails" of the crucifixion; but by three alchemical initiations which took place in the spiritual world, in the true Temple of the Rose Cross, they were able to "draw" these nails and permit the divine nature of man to come down from its cross. They concealed the processes by which this was accomplished under three alchemical metaphoric expressions: "The Casting of the Molten Sea," "The Making of the Rose Diamond," and "The Achieving of the Philosopher's Stone."

While the intellectualist flounders among contradictory theories, the mystic treats the problem in an entirely different manner. He believes that the true Rosicrucian Fraternity, consisting of a school of supermen (not unlike the fabled Mahatmas of India), is an institution existing not in the visible world bur in its spiritual counterpart, which he sees fit to call the "inner planes of Nature"; that the Brothers can be reached only by those who are capable of transcending the limitations of the material world. To substantiate their viewpoint, these mystics cite the following significant statement from the *Confessio Fraternitatis:* "A thousand times the unworthy may clamor, a thousand times may present themselves, yet God hath commanded our ears that they should hear none of them, and hath so compassed us about with His clouds that unto us, His servants, no violence can be done; wherefore now no longer are we beheld by human eyes, unless they have received strength borrowed from the eagle." In mysticism the eagle is a symbol of initiation (the spinal Spirit Fire), and by this is explained the inability of the unregenerated world to understand the Secret Order of the Rose Cross.

Those professing this theory regard the Comte de St.-Germain as their highest adept and assert that he and Christian Rosencreutz were one and the same individual. They accept fire as their universal symbol because it was the one element by means of which they could control the metals. They declared themselves the descendants of Tubal-cain and Hiram Abiff, and that the purpose of their existence was to preserve the spiritual nature of man through ages of materiality. "The Gnostic sects, the Arabs, Alchemists, Templars, Rosicrucians, and lastly the Freemasons, form the Western chain in the transmission of occult science." (See *The Tarot of the Bohemians* translated by A. E. Waite from the French of Papus.)

Max Heindel, the Christian mystic, described the Rosicrucian Temple as an "etheric structure" located in and around the home of a European country gentleman. He believed that this invisible building would ultimately be moved to the American continent. Mr. Heindel referred to the Rosicrucian

Initiates as so advanced in the science of life that "death had forgotten them."

Freemasons and Rosicrucians
The Enlightened

Rosicrucian Doctrines and Tenets
(1928)

TRUSTWORTHY information is unavailable concerning the actual philosophical beliefs, political aspirations, and humanitarian activities of the Rosicrucian Fraternity. Today, as of old, the mysteries of the Society are preserved inviolate by virtue of their essential nature; and attempts to interpret Rosicrucian philosophy are but speculations, anything to the contrary notwithstanding.

Evidence points to the probable existence of two distinct Rosicrucian bodies: an inner organization whose members never revealed their identity or teachings to the world, and an outer body under the supervision of the inner group. In all probability, the symbolic tomb of Christian Rosencreutz, Knight of the Golden Stone, was in reality this outer body, the spirit of which is in a more exalted sphere. For a period of more than a century subsequent to 1614, the outer body circulated tracts and manifestos under either its own name or the names of various initiated members. The purpose of these writings was apparently to confuse and mislead investigators, and thus effectively to conceal the actual designs of the Fraternity.

When Rosicrucianism became the philosophical "fad" of the seventeenth century, numerous documents on the subject were also circulated for purely commercial purposes by impostors desirous of capitalizing its popularity. The cunningly contrived artifices of the Fraternity itself and the blundering literary impostures of charlatans formed a double veil behind which the inner organization carried on its activities in a manner totally dissimilar to its purposes and principles as publicly disseminated. The Fratres Rosa Crucis naively refer to the misunderstandings which they have for obvious reasons permitted to exist concerning themselves as being "clouds" within which they labor and behind which they are concealed.

An inkling of the substance of Rosicrucianism—its esoteric doctrines—can be gleaned from an analysis of its shadow—its exoteric writings. In one of the most important of their "clouds," the *Confessio Fraternitatis,* the Brethren of the Fraternity of R.C. seek to justify their existence and explain (?) the purposes and activities of their Order. In its original form the *Confessio* is divided into fourteen chapters, which are here epitomized.

Confessio Fraternitatis R. C. ad Eruditos Europæ

Chapter I. Do not through hasty judgment or prejudice misinterpret the statements concerning our Fraternity published in our previous manifesto—the *Fama Fraternitatis.* Jehovah, beholding the decadence of civilization, seeks to redeem humanity by revealing to the willing and by thrusting upon the reluctant those secrets which previously He had reserved for His elect. By this wisdom the godly shall be saved, but the sorrows of the ungodly shall be multiplied. While the true purpose of our Order was set forth in the *Fama Fraternitatis,* misunderstandings have arisen through which we have been falsely accused of heresy and treason. In this document we hope so to clarify our position that the learned of Europe will be moved to join with us in the dissemination of divine knowledge according to the will of our illustrious founder.

Chapter II. While it is alleged by many that the philosophy of our day is sound, we declare it to be false and soon to die of its own inherent weakness. Just as Nature, however, provides a remedy for each new disease that manifests itself, so our Fraternity has provided a remedy for the infirmities of the world's philosophic system. The secret philosophy of the R.C. is founded upon that knowledge which is the sum and head of all faculties, sciences, and arts. By our divinely revealed system—which partakes much of theology and medicine but little of jurisprudence—we analyze the heavens and the earth; but mostly we study man himself, within whose nature is concealed the supreme secret. If the learned of out day will accept our invitation and join themselves to our Fraternity, we will reveal to them undreamed of secrets and wonders concerning the hidden workings of Nature.

Chapter III. Do not believe that the secrets discussed in this brief document are lightly esteemed by us. We cannot describe fully the marvels of our Fraternity lest the uninformed be overwhelmed by our astonishing declarations and the vulgar ridicule the mysteries which they do not comprehend. We also fear that many will be confused by the unexpected generosity of our proclamation, for not understanding the wonders of this sixth age they do nor realize the great changes which are to come. Like blind men living in a world full of light, they discern only through the sense of feeling. [By *sight* is implied spiritual cognition: by *feeling*, the material senses.]

Chapter IV. We firmly believe that through deep meditation on the inventions of the human mind and the mysteries of life, through the cooperation of the angels and spirits, and through experience and long observation, our loving Christian Father C.R.C. was so fully illumined with God's wisdom that were all the books and writings of the world lost and the foundations of science overturned, the Fraternity of R.C. could reestablish the structure of world thought upon the foundation of divine truth and integrity. Because of the great depth and perfection of our knowledge, those desiring to understand the mysteries of the Fraternity of R. C. cannot attain that wisdom immediately, but must grow in understanding and knowledge. Therefore, our Fraternity is divided into grades through which each must ascend step by step to the Great Arcanum. Now that it has pleased God to lighten unto us His sixth candelabrum, is it not better to seek truth in this way than to wander through the labyrinths of worldly ignorance?

Furthermore, those who receive this knowledge shall become masters of all arts and crafts; no secret shall be hidden from them; and all good works of the past, present, and future shall be accessible to them. The whole world shall become as one book and the contradictions of science and theology shall be reconciled. Rejoice, O humanity! for the time has come when God has decreed that the number of our Fraternity shall be increased, a labor that we have joyously undertaken. The doors of wisdom are now open to the world, but only to those who have earned the privilege may the Brothers present themselves, for it is forbidden to reveal our knowledge even to our own children. The right to receive spiritual truth cannot be inherited: it must be evolved within the soul of man himself.

Chapter V. Though we may be accused of indiscretion in offering our treasures so freely and promiscuously—without discriminating between the godly, the wise, the prince, the peasant—we affirm that we have not betrayed our trust; for although we have published our *Fama* in five languages, only those understand it who have that right. Our Society is not to be discovered by curiosity seekers, but only by serious and consecrated thinkers; nevertheless, we have circulated our *Fama* in five mother tongues so that the righteous of all nations may have an opportunity to know of us, even though they be not scholars. A thousand times the unworthy may present themselves and clamor at the gates, but God has forbidden us of the Fraternity of R.C. to hear their voices, and He has surrounded us with His clouds and His protection so that no harm may come to us, and God has decreed that we of the Order of R.C. can no longer be seen by mortal eyes unless they have received strength borrowed from the eagle. We further affirm that we shall reform the governments of Europe and pattern them according to the system applied by the philosophers of Damcar. All men desirous of securing knowledge shall receive as much as they are capable of understanding. The rule of false theology shall be overthrown and God shall make His will known through His chosen philosophers.

Chapter VII. Because of the need of brevity, it is enough to say that our Father C.R.C. was born in the year 1378 and departed at the age of 106, leaving to us the labor of spreading the doctrine of philosophic religion to the entire world. Our Fraternity is open to all who sincerely seek for truth; but we publicly warn the false and impious that they cannot betray or injure us, for God has protected our Fraternity, and all who seek to do it harm shall have their evil designs return and destroy them, while the treasures of our Fraternity shall remain untouched, to be used by the Lion in the establishment of his kingdom.

Chapter VII. We declare that God, before the end of the world, shall create a great flood of spiritual light to alleviate the sufferings of humankind. Falsehood and darkness which have crept into the arts, sciences, religions, and governments of humanity—making it difficult for even the wise to discover the path of reality—shall be forever removed and a single standard established, so that all may enjoy the fruitage of truth. We shall not be recognized as those responsible for this change, for people shall say that it is the result of the progressiveness of the age. Great are the reforms about to take place; but we of the Fraternity of R.C. do not claim to ourselves the glory for this divine reformation, since many there are, not members of our Fraternity but honest, true and wise men, who by their intelligence and their writings shall hasten its coming. We testify that sooner the stones shall rise up and offer their services than that there shall be any lack of righteous persons to execute the will of God upon earth.

Chapter VIII. That no one may doubt, we declare that God has sent messengers and signs in the heavens, namely, the new stars in *Serpentarius* and *Cygnus,* to show that a great Council of the Elect is to take place. This proves that God reveals in visible nature—for the discerning few—signs and symbols of all things that are coming to pass. God has given man two eyes, two nostrils, and two ears, but only one tongue. Whereas the eyes, the nostrils, and the ears admit the wisdom of Nature into the mind, the tongue alone may give it forth. In various ages there have been illumined ones who have seen, smelt, tasted, or heard the will of God, but it will shortly come to pass that those who have seen, smelt, tasted, or heard shall speak, and truth shall be revealed. Before this revelation of righteousness is possible, however, the world must sleep away the intoxication of her poisoned chalice (filled with the false life of the theological vine) and, opening her heart to virtue and understanding, welcome the rising sun of Truth.

Chapter IX. We have a magic writing, copied from that divine alphabet with which God writes His will upon the face of celestial and terrestrial Nature. With this new language we read God's will for all His creatures, and just as astronomers predict eclipses so we prognosticate the obscurations of the church and how long they shall last. Our language is like unto that of Adam and Enoch before the Fall, and though we understand and can explain our mysteries in this our sacred language, we cannot do so in Latin, a tongue contaminated by the confusion of Babylon.

Chapter X. Although there are still certain powerful persons who oppose and hinder us—because of which we must remain concealed—we exhort those who would become of our Fraternity to study unceasingly the Sacred Scriptures, for such as do this cannot be far from us. We do not mean that the Bible should be continually in the mouth of man, but that he should search for its true and eternal meaning, which is seldom discovered by theologians, scientists, or mathematicians because they are blinded by the opinions of their sects. We bear witness that never since the beginning of the world has there been given to man a more excellent book than the Holy Bible. Blessed is he who possesses it, more blessed he who reads it, most blessed he who understands it, and most godlike he who obeys it.

Chapter XI. We wish the statements we made in the *Fama Fraternitatis* concerning the transmutation of metals and the universal medicine to be lightly understood. While we realize that both these works are attainable by man, we fear that many really great minds may be led away from the true quest of knowledge and understanding if they permit themselves to limit their investigation to the transmutation of metals. When to a man is given power to heal disease, to overcome poverty, and to reach a position of worldly dignity, that man is beset by numerous temptations and unless he possess true knowledge and full understanding he will become a terrible menace to mankind. The alchemist who attains to the art of transmuting base metals can do all manner of evil unless his understanding be as great as his self-created wealth. We therefore affirm that man must first gain knowledge, virtue, and understanding; then all other things may be added unto him. We accuse the Christian Church of the great sin of possessing power and using it unwisely; therefore, we prophesy that it shall fall by the weight of its own iniquities and its crown shall be brought to naught.

Chapter XII. In concluding our *Confessio,* we earnestly admonish you to cast aside the worthless books of pseudo-alchemists and philosophers (of whom there are many in our age), who make light of the Holy Trinity and deceive the credulous with meaningless enigmas. One of the greatest of these is a stage player, a man with sufficient ingenuity for imposition. Such men are mingled by the Enemy of human welfare among those who seek to do good, thus making Truth more difficult of discovery. Believe us, Truth is simple and unconcealed, while falsehood is complex, deeply hidden, proud, and its worldly knowledge, seemingly a glitter with godly luster, is often mistaken for divine wisdom. You that are wise will turn from these false teachings and come to us, who seek not your money but freely offer you our greater treasure. We desire not your goods, but that you should become partakers of our goods. We do not deride parables but invite you to understand all parables and all secrets. We do not ask you to receive us, but invite you to come unto our kingly houses and palaces, not because of ourselves but because we are so ordered by the Spirit of God, the desire of our most excellent Father C.R.C., and the need of the present moment, which is very great.

Chapter XIII. Now that we have made our position clear that we sincerely confess Christ; disavow the Papacy; devote our lives to true philosophy and worthy living; and daily invite and admit into our Fraternity the worthy of all nations, who thereafter share with us the Light of God: will you not join yourselves with us to the perfection of yourselves, the development of all the arts, and the service of the world? If you will take this step, the treasures of every part of the earth shall be at one time given unto you, and the darkness which envelopes human knowledge and which results in the vanities of material arts and sciences shall be forever dispelled.

Chapter XIV. Again we warn those who are dazzled by the glitter of gold or those who, now upright, might be turned by great riches to a life of idleness and pomp, not to disturb our sacred silence with their clamorings; for though there be a medicine which will cure all diseases and give unto all men wisdom, yet it is against the will of God that men should attain to understanding by any means other than virtue, labor, and integrity. We are not permitted to manifest ourselves to any man except it be by the will of God. Those who believe that they can partake of our spiritual wealth against the will of God or without His sanction will find that they shall sooner lose their lives in seeking us than attain happiness by finding us.

FRATERNITAS R.C.

Johann Valentin Andreæ is generally reputed to be the author of the *Confessio*. It is a much-mooted question, however, whether Andreæ did not permit his name to be used as a pseudonym by Sir Francis Bacon. Apropos of this subject are two extremely significant references occurring in the introduction to that remarkable potpourri, *The Anatomy of Melancholy*. This volume first appeared in 1621 from the pen of Democritus junior, who was afterwards identified as Robert Burton, who, in turn, was a suspected intimate of Sir Francis Bacon. One reference archly suggests that at the time of publishing *The Anatomy of Melancholy* in 1621 the founder of the Fraternity of R.C. was still alive. This statement—concealed from general recognition by its textual involvement—has escaped the notice of most students of Rosicrucianism. In the same work there also appears a short footnote of stupendous import. It contains merely the words: "Job. Valent. Andreas, Lord Verulam." This single line definitely relates Johann Valentin Andreæ to Sir Francis Bacon, who was Lord Verulam, and by its punctuation intimates that they are one and the same individual.

Prominent among Rosicrucian apologists was John Heydon, who inscribes himself "A Servant of God, and a Secretary of Nature." In his curious work, *The Rosie Cross Uncovered*, he gives an enigmatic but valuable description of the Fraternity of R.C. in the following language:

"Now there are a kind of men, as they themselves report, named *Rosie Crucians*, a divine fraternity that inhabit the suburbs of heaven, and these are the officers of the *Generalissimo* of the world, that are as the eyes and ears of the great King, seeing and hearing all things: they say these *Rosie Crucians* are seraphically illuminated, as Moses was, according to this order of the elements, earth refin'd to water, water to air, air to fire." He further declares that these mysterious Brethren possessed polymorphous powers, appearing in any desired form at will. In the preface of the same work, he enumerates the strange powers of the Rosicrucian adepts:

"I shall here tell you what *Rosie Crucians* are, and that *Moses* was their Father; some say they were of the order of Elias, some say the Disciples of Ezekiel; [...] For it should seem *Rosie Crucians* were not only initiated into the Mosaical Theory, but have arrived also to the power of working miracles, as *Moses, Elias, Ezekiel*, and the succeeding Prophets did, as being transported where they please, as *Habakkuk* was from *Jewry* to Babylon, or as Philip, after he had baptized the *Eunuch* to Azorus, and one of these went from me to a friend of mine in Devonshire, and came and brought me an answer to London the someday, which is four days journey; they caught me excellent predictions of Astrology and Earthquakes; they slack the Plague in Cities; they silence the violent Winds and Tempests; they calm the rage of the Sea and Rivers; they walk in the Air, they frustrate the malicious aspects of Witches; they cure all Diseases."

The writings of John Heydon are considered a most important contribution to Rosicrucian literature. John Heydon was probably related to Sir Christopher Heydon, "a Seraphically Illuminated *Rosie Crucian,* " whom the late F. Leigh Gardner, Hon. Secretary Sec. Ros. in Anglia, believes to have been the source of his Rosicrucian knowledge. In his *Bibliotheca Rosicrucian*a he makes the following statement concerning John Heydon: "On the whole, from the internal evidence of his writings, he appears to have gone through the lower grade of the R. C. Order and to have given out much of this to the world." John Heydon traveled extensively, visiting Arabia, Egypt, Persia, and various parts of Europe, as related in a biographical introduction to his work, *The Wise-Mans Crown, Set with Angels, Planets, Metals, etc.,* or *The Glory of the Rosie Cross*—a work declared by him to be a translation into English of the mysterious book *M* brought from Arabia by Christian Rosencreutz.

Thomas Vaughan (Eugenius Philalethes), another champion of the Order, corroborates the statement of John Heydon concerning the ability of the Rosicrucian initiates to make themselves invisible at will: "The Fraternity of R.C. can move in this white mist. 'Whosoever would communicate with us must be able to see in this light, or us he will never see unless by our own will.'"

The Fraternity of R.C. is an august and sovereign body, arbitrarily manipulating the symbols of alchemy, Qabbalism, astrology, and magic to the attainment of its own peculiar purposes, but entirely independent of the cults whose terminology it employs. The three major objects of the Fraternity are:

1. *The abolition of all monarchical forms of government and the substitution therefor of the rulership of the philosophic elect.* The present democracies are the direct outgrowth of Rosicrucian efforts to liberate the maws from the domination of

despotism. In the early part of the eighteenth century the Rosicrucians turned their attention to the new American Colonies, then forming the nucleus of a great nation in the New World. The American War of Independence represents their first great political experiment and resulted in the establishment of a national government founded upon the fundamental principles of divine and natural law. As an imperishable reminder of their *sub rosa* activities, the Rosicrucians left the Great Seal of the United States. The Rosicrucians were also the instigators of the French Revolution, but in this instance were not wholly successful, owing to the fact that the fanaticism of the revolutionists could not be controlled, and the Reign of Terror ensued.

2. *The reformation of science, philosophy, and ethics.* The Rosicrucians declared that the material arts and sciences were but shadows of the divine wisdom, and that only by penetrating the innermost recesses of Nature could man attain to reality and understanding. Though calling themselves Christians, the Rosicrucians were evidently Platonists and also profoundly versed in the deepest mysteries of early Hebrew and Hindu theology. There is undeniable evidence that the Rosicrucians desired to reestablish the institutions of the ancient Mysteries as the foremost method of instructing humanity in the secret and eternal doctrine. Indeed, being in all probability the perpetuators of the ancient Mysteries, the Rosicrucians were able to maintain themselves against the obliterating forces of dogmatic Christianity only by absolute secrecy and the subtlety of their subterfuges. They so carefully guarded and preserved the Supreme Mystery—the identity and interrelationship of the *Three Selves*—that no one to whom they did not of their own accord reveal themselves has ever secured any satisfactory information regarding either the existence or the purpose of the Order. The Fraternity of R.C., through its outer organization, is gradually creating an environment or body in which the Illustrious Brother C.R.C. may ultimately incarnate and consummate for humanity the vast spiritual and material labors of the Fraternity.

3. *The discovery of the Universal Medicine, or panacea, for all forms of disease.* There is ample evidence that the Rosicrucians were successful in their quest for the Elixir of Life. In his *Theatrum Chemicum Britannicum,* Elias Ashmole states that the Rosicrucians were not appreciated in England, but were welcomed on the Continent. He also states that Queen Elizabeth was twice cured of the smallpox by the Brethren of the Rosy Cross, and that the Earl of Norfolk was healed of leprosy by a Rosicrucian physician. In the quotations that follow it is. hinted by John Heydon that the Brothers of the Fraternity possessed the secret of prolonging human existence indefinitely, but not beyond the time appointed by the will of God:

"And at last they could restore by the same course every Brother that died to life again, and so continue many ages; the rules you find in the fourth book. [...] After this manner began the Fraternity of the Rosie Cross, first by four persons, who died and rose again until Christ, and then they came to worship as the Star guided them to Bethlehem of Judea, where lay our Savior in his mother's arms; and then they opened their treasure and presented unto him gifts, gold, frankincense, and myrrh, and by the commandment of God went home to their habitation. These four waxing young again successively many hundreds of years, made a magical language and writing, with a large dictionary, which we yet daily use to God's praise and glory, and do find great wisdom therein. [...] Now whilst Brother C.R. was in a proper womb quickening, they concluded to draw and receive yet others more into their Fraternity."

The *womb* herein referred to was apparently the glass casket, or container, in which the Brothers were buried. This was also called the *philosophical egg.* After a certain period of time the philosopher, breaking the shell of his egg, came forth and functioned for a prescribed period, after which he retired again into his shell of glass. The Rosicrucian medicine for the healing of all human infirmities may be interpreted either as a chemical substance which produces the physical effects described or as spiritual understanding—the true healing power which, when a man has partaken of it, reveals truth to him. Ignorance is the worst form of disease, and that: which heals ignorance is therefore the most potent of all medicines. The perfect Rosicrucian medicine was for the healing of nations, races, and individuals.

In an early unpublished manuscript, an unknown philosopher declares alchemy, Qabbalism, astrology, and magic to have been divine sciences originally, but that through perversion they had become false doctrines, leading seekers after wisdom ever farther from their goal. The same author gives a valuable key to esoteric Rosicrucianism by dividing the path of spiritual attainment into three steps, or schools, which he calls *mountains*. The first and lowest of these mountains is *Mount Sophia;* the second, *Mount Qabbalah;* and the third, *Mount Magia*. These three mountains are sequential stages of spiritual growth. The unknown author then states:

"By philosophy is to be understood the knowledge of the workings of Nature, by which knowledge man learns to climb to those higher mountains above the limitations of sense. By Qabbalism is to be understood the language of the angelic or celestial beings, and he who masters it is able to converse with the messengers of God. On the highest of the mountains is the School of Magia (Divine Magic, which is the language of God) wherein man is taught the true nature of all things by God Himself."

There is a growing conviction that if the true nature of Rosicrucianism were divulged, it would cause consternation, to say the least. Rosicrucian symbols have many meanings, but the Rosicrucian meaning has not yet been revealed. The mount upon which stands the House of the Rosy Cross is still concealed by clouds, in which the Brethren hide both themselves and their secrets. Michael Maier writes: "What is contained in the *Fama* and *Confessio* is true. It is a very childish objection that the brotherhood have promised so much and performed so little. With them, as elsewhere, many are called but few are chosen. The masters of the order hold out the rose as the remote prize, but they impose the cross on those who are entering." (See

Silentium post Clamores, by Maier, and *The Rosicrucians and the Freemasons,* by De Quincey.)

The rose and the cross appear upon the stained-glass windows of Lichfield Chapter House, where Walter Conrad Arensberg believes Lord Bacon and his mother to have been buried. A crucified rose within a heart is watermarked into the dedication page of the 1628 edition of Robert Burton's *Anatomy of Melancholy.*

The fundamental symbols of the Rosicrucians were the rose and the cross; the rose female and the cross male, both universal phallic emblems. While such learned gentlemen as Thomas Inman, Hargrave Jennings, and Richard Payne Knight have truly observed that the rose and the cross typify the generative processes, these scholars seem unable to pierce the veil of symbolism; they do not realize that the creative mystery in the material world is merely a shadow of the divine creative mystery in the spiritual world. Because of the phallic significance of their symbols, both the Rosicrucians and the Templars have been falsely accused of practicing obscene rites in their secret ceremonials. While it is quite true that the alchemical retort symbolizes the womb, it also has a far more significant meaning concealed under the allegory of the second birth. As generation is the key to material existence, it is natural that the Fraternity of R.C. should adopt as its characteristic symbols those exemplifying the reproductive processes. As regeneration is the key to spiritual existence, they therefore founded their symbolism upon the rose and the cross, which typify the redemption of man through the union of his lower temporal nature with his higher eternal nature. The rosy cross is also a hieroglyphic figure representing the formula of the Universal Medicine.

Thank you for buying this Cornerstone book!

For over 25 years now, I've tried to provide the Masonic community with quality books on Masonic education, philosophy, and general interest. Your support means everything to us and keeps us afloat. Cornerstone is by no means a large company. We are a small family-owned operation that depends on your support.

Please visit our website and have a look at the many books we offer as well as the different categories of books.

If your lodge, Grand Lodge, research lodge, book club, or other body would like to have quality Cornerstone books to sell or distribute, write us. We can give you outstanding books, prices, and service.

Thanks again!
Michael R. Poll
Publisher

Cornerstone Book Publishers
1cornerstonebooks@gmail.com
http://cornerstonepublishers.com

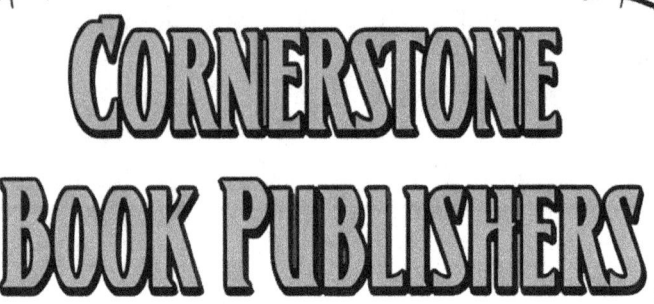

More Books from Cornerstone

Living Freemasonry
A Better Path to Travel
by Michael R. Poll
6x9 Softcover 180 pages
ISBN 99781934935958

The Doctrine of Charity and Faith
by Emanuel Swedenborg
Translated by T. B. Hayward
6x9 Softcover 112 pages
ISBN 1613422865

10,000 Famous Freemasons
4 Vol. Softcover Edition
by William Denslow
Foreword by Harry S. Truman
Cornerstone Foreword by Michael R. Poll
8.5 x 11, Softcover 2 Volumes 1,515 pages
ISBN 1887560319

The Rose Cross Order
by R. Swinburne Clymer
6×9 Softcover 212 pages
ISBN: 1613422830

The Scottish Rite Papers
A Study of the Troubled History of the Louisiana and US Scottish Rite in the Early to Mid-1800s
by Michael R. Poll
6x9 Softcover 240 pages
ISBN 9781613423448

Cornerstone Book Publishers
www.cornerstonepublishers.com

More Books from Cornerstone

The Astral Plane
By C. W. Leadbeater
Foreword by Evelyn Klebert
6×9 Softcover 136 pages
ISBN: 978-1934935996

Rosicrucian Trio
The Rosicrucian Manifestos
Fama Fraternitatis, Confessio Fraternitatis and Chymical Wedding of Christian Rosenkreutz
Introduction by Michael R. Poll
6×9 Softcover 128 pages
ISBN: 978-1-61342-326-4

The Particular Nature of Freemasons
by Michael R. Poll
6x9 Softcover 156 pages
ISBN 9781613423462

The Ancient Wisdom
by Annie Besant
6x9 Softcover 178 pages
ISBN 1934935085

An Encyclopedia of Freemasonry
by Albert Mackey
Revised by William J. Hughan and Edward L. Hawkins
Foreword by Michael R. Poll
8.5 x 11, Softcover 2 Volumes 960 pages
ISBN 1613422520

Cornerstone Book Publishers
www.cornerstonepublishers.com

More Books from Cornerstone

The Symbolism of Colour
by Ellen Conroy
6×9 Softcover 80 pages
ISBN: 1613420838

The Canon
An Exposition of the Pagan Mystery Perpetuated in the Cabala as the Rule of All Arts
by William Stirling
6×9 Softcover 428 pages
ISBN: 1613420854

Manual of the Eastern Star
by Rob Morris
foreword by Jonathan K. Poll
6×9 Softcover 128 pages
ISBN: 978-1613422946

Egyptian Masonic Rite of Memphis
by Calvin C. Burt
6x9 Softcover 352 pages
ISBN 1613420455

The History of Magic
by Eliphas Levi
Translated by A. E. Waite
6x9 Softcover 594 pages
ISBN 1613421559

Cornerstone Book Publishers
www.cornerstonepublishers.com

More Books from Cornerstone

The Brotherhood of the Rosy Cross
by E. Waite
6×9 Softcover 652 pages
ISBN: 1613420013

Morals and Dogma of the Scottish Rite Craft Degrees
by Albert Pike
foreword by Michael R. Poll
6×9 Softcover 152 pages
ISBN: 1887560866

The Newly-Made Mason
by H. L. Haywood
Revised by Michael R. Poll
6×9 Softcover 188 pages
ISBN: 9781613423578

Cross' Masonic Chart
by Jeremy L. Cross
Edited by William M. Cunningham
6x9 Softcover 330 pages
ISBN 9781613423004

Illustrations of Masonry
by William Preston
Additions by George Oliver
Foreword by Michael R. Poll
6x9 Softcover 404 pages
ISBN 9781613423530

Cornerstone Book Publishers
www.cornerstonepublishers.com

More Books from Cornerstone

The Doctrine and Literature of the Kabalah
by A.E. Waite
6x9 Softcover 536 pages
ISBN 1613422393

Outline of the Rise and Progress of Freemasonry in Louisiana
by James B. Scot
Edited by Robert L. Poll
Introduction by Alain Bernheim
Afterword by Michael R. Poll
8x10 Softcover 180 pages
ISBN 1-934935-31-X

Numbers
Their Occult Power and Mystic Virtues
W. Wynn Westcott
6 x 9 Softcover 140 pages
ISBN: 1934935555

Zanoni
A Rosicrucian Tale
by Edward Bulwer Lytton
6 x 9 Softcover 306 pages
ISBN 161342051X

Robert's Rules of Order: Masonic Edition
Revised by Michael R. Poll
6 x 9 Softcover 212 pages
ISBN 1887560076

Cornerstone Book Publishers
www.cornerstonepublishers.com

More Books from Cornerstone

Occult Science in Medicine
by Franz Hartmann
6 x 9 Softcover 110 pages
ISBN: 1613421133

The Ancient and Accepted Scottish Rite in Thirty-Three Degrees
by Robert B. Folger
Introduction by Michael R. Poll
ISBN: 1934935883

The Initiates of the Flame
by Manly P. Hall
6x9 Softcover 96 pages
ISBN: 1613421990

Francis Bacon and His Secret Society
by Constance M. Pott
6 x 9 Softcover 426 pages
ISBN: 1934935182

The Five Senses
by Emanuel Swendenborg
Translated by Enoch S. Price
6x9 Softcover 320 pages
ISBN: 1613422822

Brother of the Third Degree
by Will L. Garver
6 x 9 Softcover 228 pages
ISBN: 1887560432

Cornerstone Book Publishers
www.cornerstonepublishers.com

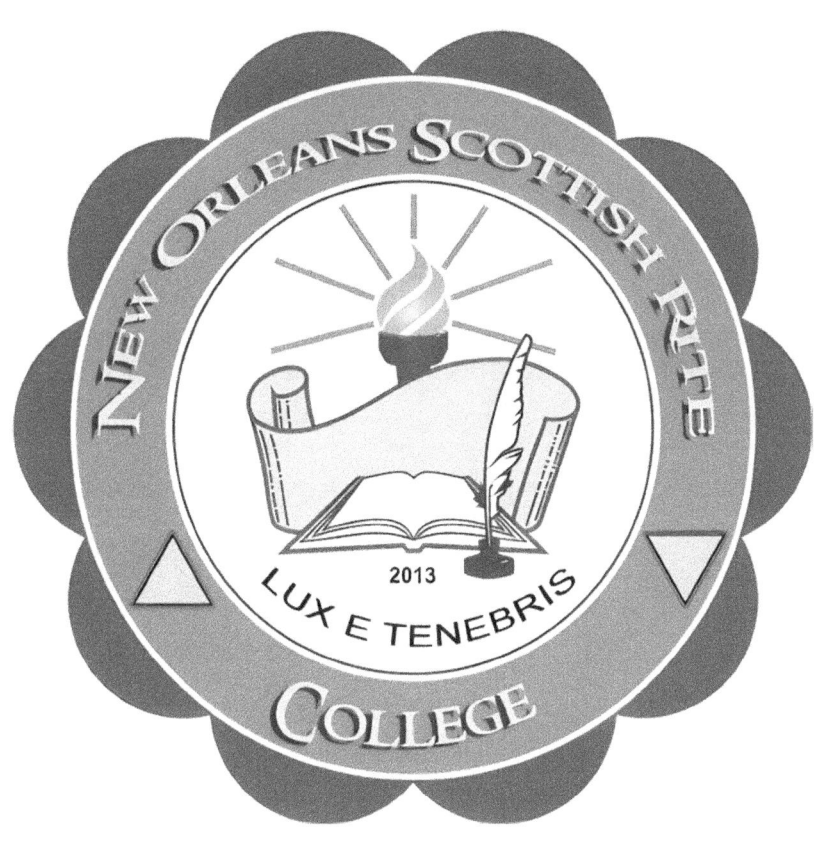

New Orleans Scottish Rite College

www.youtube.com/c/NewOrleansScottishRiteCollege

Clear, Easy to Watch
Scottish Rite and Craft Lodge
Podcast & Video Education

www.ingramcontent.com/pod-product-compliance
Lightning Source LLC
LaVergne TN
LVHW021825060526
838201LV00058B/3505